T0209324

THE ROAD OF MIRACLES

The Methods to Remove All Worries in the World

CHONG WEIQIANG,
HUANG HAI

BALBOA.PRESS
A DIVISION OF HAY HOUSE

Balboa Press books may be ordered through booksellers or by contacting:

Balboa Press
A Division of Hay House
1663 Liberty Drive
Bloomington, IN 47403
www.balboapress.com
844-682-1282

Because of the dynamic nature of the Internet, any web addresses or links contained in this book may have changed since publication and may no longer be valid. The views expressed in this work are solely those of the author and do not necessarily reflect the views of the publisher, and the publisher hereby disclaims any responsibility for them.

The author of this book does not dispense medical advice or prescribe the use of any technique as a form of treatment for physical, emotional, or medical problems without the advice of a physician, either directly or indirectly. The intent of the author is only to offer information of a general nature to help you in your quest for emotional and spiritual well-being. In the event you use any of the information in this book for yourself, which is your constitutional right, the author and the publisher assume no responsibility for your actions.

Any people depicted in stock imagery provided by Getty Images are models, and such images are being used for illustrative purposes only. Certain stock imagery © Getty Images.

Print information available on the last page.

ISBN: 978-1-9822-5006-5 (sc)
ISBN: 978-1-9822-5008-9 (hc)
ISBN: 978-1-9822-5007-2 (e)

Library of Congress Control Number: 2020911774

Balboa Press rev. date: 10/20/2020

A Voice from beyond Dream

A voice sneaks into my dream I surmise as fantasy
Awakens me to behold Jesus glowing with a smiling face
Reminiscent of lilies blooming in heavenly home
Sacred fragrances pervade the holy infinity
Glittering tears still linger on my eyelashes
While a Cordial regard comes from Jesus
'Father has demolished all hurdles for you
Image of your back is inscribed with Father's concern
During the instant of your absence from his Bosom'
The last speck of angst slips in quiet from palm
Homestead's rainbow ascends to dazzling clear sky
Pure Lilies held in hands of Brothers
Whose Innocent cheeks overflow with joy
Myriads of cantos insuffice to convey grandeur and freedom
of our heavenly home
Let's dance in unified joy
with hairs suffering the elements no more

A voice sneaks into my dream I surmise as fantasy
Awakens me to behold Jesus glowing with a smiling face

Contents

Q & A OF MIRACLES (PART III)

Preface

I wrote this message just to speak for the truth, and all of these voices came from 'A Course in Miracles'. Therefore, this book can be called a guide to the actual practices of 'A Course in Miracles'. Of course, as an author, I am only one of the sons and daughters of God. So I'm just one of the speakers of 'A Course in Miracles'. However, I hope you can embark on the road of miracles by reading this book. This book really relies on a website and echoes it remotely. And this website relies on the spiritual therapists of miracles who have bodies, and echoes them remotely. So this book is not only "alive", but also "alive" forever, because more and more therapists will appear on the website. And these therapists will ensure that the will of the Holy Spirit is passed on from generation to generation. The website address is: www.miraclestaiwan.com

About the contents of this book:

1. Chapter 1 and Chapter 2 of Required Readings (Part I) are for the general public. These two pieces of information will outline your mind's memory that exceeds the ultimate limit.

2. In the middle chapters of Required Readings (Part I) the application of several important thinking modes in 'A Course in Miracles' is described. You can use these narrations to practice miracle minds in real life.

3. The last chapter of Required Readings (Part I) points out the pure rules that spiritual therapists of miracles should follow, which can give you directions.

4. All the information in Part II comes from Ann's psychic works, which not only has a gentle healing effect on your mind, but also helps you complete the reading of the first half.

5. Questions and Answers on Miracles (Part III) answer some general problems that you may encounter in the course of spiritual practices.

6. The function of the appendix is to connect the book with the main text "A Course in Miracles".

Finally, the author is willing to open the great "age of miracles" with you and everyone.

REQUIRED READINGS (PART I)

1 The Birth of the Universe and the Truth about "Me" (The Foundational Chapter)

The worries in the world can be divided into several types:

1. You feel deprived and fearful because of failing to get certain things and relationships.

2. You want to change your destiny and change others, but you can't. So, you often live in the pain of hate and self-hatred.

3. When you have gotten some things and relationships that satisfy you, you find such satisfaction doesn't last long. Then, you go on to pursue new goals, and end up in a cycle of "seek but not find" things that will constantly satisfy you.

4. Sometimes you feel that you give too much to others, but you get too little and you can't change anything, so you have to endure the situation exhaustedly.

5. Your fear of the future, illness and death.

In short, there are so many worries in the world. I will not explain them one by one, for I am going to illustrate how to remove them.

In order to remove all the worries in the world, you need to have a basic understanding, that is, you need to understand the answers to several mysteries in the world. These mysteries can be summarized as follows:

1. How did this vast universe come about?
2. What is the meaning of my life?
3. Who am I?
4. Where do I come from and where do I go?

The answers to these questions are the basis for removing all worries in the world. I won't talk about how scientists and biologists answer these mysteries. I'll directly go into the subject to illustrate the answers to these mysteries.

First, I will take you into an imaginary space with words, so you can begin to imagine with them:

We have all taken baths in a thermal basin, and there are many hot springs in the world. Imagine the feeling that you are soaking in an infinite hot spring. Such feeling must be very warm, comfortable, and cozy. And then, further imagine, if you became a drop of water in the hot spring, what would you feel? You will feel the following points:

1. You, a drop of water, are integrated with the entire hot spring, and you are also integrated with an infinite number of other water drops. So, you first feel that you are the hot spring.

2. You feel completely safe, because this hot spring is infinite. The hot spring is infinite, so you know you will not leave the whole hot spring.

3. You feel you have nothing to ask for and nothing to want. Because there is nothing else to do for a drop of water. All you can do is simply enjoy the warmth and comfort of the entire hot spring.

These are some important feelings you have as a drop of water in the hot spring. Next, I will continue to personalize this drop of water. When this little water drop was experiencing the warmth and comfort of the hot spring in a carefree manner, an emergency situation suddenly appeared, which is that this little water drop had an idea in a moment, and this idea is similar to "what if I develop by myself outside the hot spring?". With the emergence of this idea, this drop of water got into a kind of absent-minded state.

For the absent-minded state, I think everyone has experienced it. For example, when students are in class, they are distracted while listening. For me, I liked playing football in school. Sometimes I would have an idea in class, "What would it be like if I was playing football in the field right now?" Then, I would get into a fantasy space, imagining how I would play on the field, and how I would dribble and shoot. Sometimes when my teacher saw that I was distracted, he would throw chalk at my face, and then it dawned on me that I was in class and wasn't playing football on the playground at all. Sometimes, because of hot weather, I would be distracted in class. I would imagine I was under the shade of trees to enjoy the coolness. I think we all have had such mind wandering before, so I won't explain it further. But the key point of mind wandering is that no matter how absent-minded I was in class; I definitely didn't leave the classroom.

It is true with this little water drop too. When he came up with the thought "what if I would develop myself outside of hot spring…", he entered an absent-minded state, which led to a major change in his properties in the first place. The property of the water drop used to be pure experience and pure enjoyment. He had been experiencing the warmth and comfort of the hot spring. But when he was distracted by that little thought, something new appeared. It was intangible consciousness. The first cognition produced by this consciousness was "I, a water drop, have broken away from the hot spring". At this point, when the water drop became distracted his property changed from pure experience to consciousness. In a flash, the change also caused the water drop to lose all feelings in the hot spring. This is similar to the example I just showed. When I was distracted in class, I was playing on the playground. I immediately lost the feeling of being in the class, which is true of the little drop of water.

But after the first cognition, this water drop's consciousness did not directly enter into any fantasy space. Because the water drop only knew the existence of hot spring before wandering, and other things did not exist for him. So, when the water drop was distracted, he just stayed alone in a world with no room. During that time, this intangible water drop's consciousness produced the following thought: "how can I come out of this comfortable and safe hot spring? Can I really come out? Why do I recall enjoying pure warmth and comfort in hot spring?" There are two sounds that came to the water drop's consciousness:

1. I haven't left the hot spring, and now it's my delusion.

2. I have really got out of the hot spring and I can develop by myself.

After a battle of thought, this water drop's consciousness finally chose the second sound and decided, "I have really got out of the hot spring and will develop by myself". So far, the whole experience of the hot spring had become his memory.

This intangible water drop's consciousness kept recalling the warmth, comfort and safety he had felt in the hot spring, and he compared those feelings with his current lonely feeling. After the comparison, he found the warm, comfortable and safe feelings were gone, which made the water drop's consciousness produce a feeling it never had, a sense of deprivation. As this kind of comparison was constantly made, the sense of deprivation of the water drop's consciousness got greater and greater. Finally, because of the great sense of deprivation, he had the following fatal idea, "look at what I have done, the hot spring is so infinite, so warm and comfortable, and it takes care of me well. But I have silently gotten out of it; I have done something wrong". At this point, the water drop's consciousness realized that it was a big mistake for him to leave the hot spring, and experienced guilt and hatred.

Then, the water drop's consciousness began to think, "the hot spring must know that I left without saying goodbye, so the hot spring must be very angry now, and he will certainly not let me off. The hot spring is so strong, so I cannot beat him and will be caught by him sooner or later and destroyed. I'd better run away! Run to a place without the hot spring". The water drop's consciousness thought it was rebelling against the hot spring that he left the hot spring, So the water drop's consciousness feared revenge by the hot spring. Finally, he thought of escape because of this fear. The thought of the water drop's consciousness is similar to that of the human world: "someone has been taking special care of me, caring for me in every possible way, but I left him without a word. So, I let him down, and thoroughly offended him. And this guy will be furious with me for leaving. So I mustn't get caught by him. If I am caught, he is going to kill me.

What is the truth? The truth is that the water drop does not leave the hot spring at all. It is only after entering an absent-minded state that a series of false thoughts emerged. These false thoughts are mere illusions. Moreover, the most interesting thing is that the little water drop mistakenly thought that he left the hot spring, but the hot spring is very clear that the

4

little water drop does not leave him, so the hot spring still gives the little water drop warmth and comfort as usual. It's just that this little water drop could not experience it after getting into a state of mind wandering.

Then, the most critical step began. This water drop's consciousness that was guilt-ridden and fear-laden began to flee, and it deeply knew that there were two things to do in the process of escape. The first thing was it should drive out its inner feeling of guilt in the process of escape, because fear came from its guilty feeling;only when the guilt was driven out could it live at ease. Just like when people claim they are right and others are wrong when quarrelling, because only by putting sin and error on others can they live in peace of mind. The second thing was that it had to run to a place where there was no hot spring, and where there was no shadow of the hot spring, so that it could completely forget the hot spring and get rid of the fear of being hunted by the hot spring.

In this way, when the water drop's consciousness confirmed the two things to be completed, the earth-shaking drama of escape was staged. In the moment of his escape, the intangible water drop's consciousness simultaneously completed the following key things:

1. This intangible water drop's consciousness designed and dreamt up a world that was completely contrary to the hot spring, because it has escaped from the hot spring can be proof that its characteristics were completely contrary to those of the hot spring. the characteristics of the hot spring were oneness, constancy, infinity, intangibleness, eternity, all-embracing warmth, lack of nothing, and no opposition. The world designed by the water drop's consciousness is opposite of the hot spring, which is characterized by individuality, change, peculiarity, image, time, separation, scarcity and binary opposition. When the water drop's consciousness designed these characteristics, it can instantly imagine the world. This kind of fantasy could be called projection of illusions, which is the same as entering a fantasy world when one is distracted. So, what does this imagined world look like? The world has hundreds of billions of individual galaxies and an almost infinite number of individual bodies. Space is composed of these hundreds of billions of individual and separate

5

galaxies which corresponds to the hot spring's oneness, and the nearly infinite number of individual bodies corresponds to the infinite number of water drops with oneness in the hot spring.

2. While projecting all the galaxies and all the bodies, the water drop's consciousness expelled all guilt within it into these galaxies and bodies. Moreover, the process of expelling sins and the process of projecting all galaxies and bodies is done simultaneously. This pattern of simultaneity and synchronicity could also be stated as: when the water drop's consciousness drove out its internal guilt, this massive guilt was immediately and magically transformed into hundreds of billions of galaxies and almost infinite number of bodies.

3. When the water drop's consciousness projected all galaxies and countless bodies, a more crucial step happened, the water drop's consciousness got into a body it had projected at the same time. This body was not different from others, but this body was the most critical tool for the water drop's consciousness to drive the guilt out, because there was no difference between what was inside and what was outside for the intangible water drop's consciousness. It expelled sins, however, without an externality, it was impossible to drive out what was within. So it needed a body to completely differentiate what was inside from what was outside, and drive out the inner guilt, that is why it entered a body. Furthermore, the instant it entered the body, this intangible water drop's consciousness became a new consciousness, which was the self-consciousness. And the first cognition after the birth of the self-consciousness was "I am a new body, I am pure and innocent, what is inside my body is called the inner, what is outside my body is called the outer, and I live in a real universe". The water drop's consciousness finally used a body bound to the self-consciousness to drive out all inner guilt. At the same time, all guilt was magically transformed into a world whose characteristics were diametrically opposed to those of the hot spring, and this world was located outside the body that bound the self-consciousness. At last, the universe was born.

After the universe was born, the water drop's consciousness that had become the self-consciousness completely forgot the hot spring, and completely forgot that the universe was created by it, so he still thinks he lives in a real universe; this person is you. Whoever you are, the one who has launched the universe is you who is reading this message right now.

The above information for the birth of the universe is a simpler version. In the following, I will tell who you really are, because you are certainly not a drop of water in the hot spring, it's just a metaphor, but you can replace hot spring with a "place"; the characteristics of this "place" are oneness, intangibility, perfection, invariability, eternity, infinity, purity, integrity, richness, endless succession, all-embracing holy love, non-duality, and pure unity. This "place" is your real home. The real "you" is not a body; the real "you" is just an intangible and perfect spirit living in this home. Moreover, you, the perfect spirit, are inseparable from the home, and eternally enjoy the well-being and wealth of the whole home. It's like a drop of water living in a hot spring. And you are not alone in your home, because there is an infinite number of perfect spirits who are identical with you in the home, and they are all with you. It is like a drop of water in hot spring coexisting with countless other drops.That's the truth about you.

However, when you, the perfect spirit, are enjoying bliss in eternity, at some moment, comes up with an idea that "what if I could develop myself outside my home..." out of the blue, the prefect spirit enters a state of mind wandering. That state of mind wandering is like a small doze, entering a dreamland. Then, in the delusional dream, first you mistakenly think that you have left the blissful homeland and produce a great sense of deprivation, and then due to great guilt and fear, you project an incredibly large universe and live in it. This is all your truth. So, for the real you, you just dream of a universal space, dream of time, and dream of you being a body, dream of other bodies, dream of your birth and death, and dream of your life. That's all.

Then, I use two more examples of the human world to make a very simple illustration that the evidence for the pattern of the universe's birth can be found in the human world.

When a baby is born, do you think the baby is guilty? Absolutely not. Because he is a new body, he is guiltless. So, every person who comes into this world is bound to the body of a baby, which can show that he is a pure and innocent life. This pattern is a repeated simulation that the self-consciousness binds the body and acquires innocence at the moment of the universe's birth.

You can also think about. how everyone in the world is constantly thinking in their lives that "I'm guiltless. It's your fault". Everyone, even prison inmates, will think, "there's a reason for what I'm doing, because of social issues, or family issues, or I am forced by someone, etc., so I am innocent". Such thoughts are common because they are the constant repetitions of "driving guilt out" at the moment of the birth of the universe.

So, the pattern and connotation of the universe's birth have never disappeared in the human world, only appears in different forms. Especially in the field of human relations, if you carefully observe the conflict, you will find that the worries in the world are nothing but expelling sins to each other. That's all. Because no one wants to feel guilty, and everyone wants to live guiltlessly and innocently.

I use hot spring and water drop as a metaphor to simply illustrate the process of the birth of the universe and who you are. This brief introduction is just a stepping-stone for your learning. If you are willing to continue to learn the methods of remove all worries, you can read the next required reading message "methods to remove all the worries (basic in-depth part)". In the next part, I will use orthodox language to explain the appearance of the universe and your truth in depth.

In the end, I will simply explain how religion connects to the message of this part. If you are a Christian, you can replace 'the hot spring' with 'the Christian paradise'; if you are a Muslim, you can replace 'the hot spring' with 'the paradise of Islam'; Judaists can replace 'the hot spring' by the intangible 'true god'. There is no accurate word in Buddhism for that concept. If you are a Buddhist, you can replace the hot spring with 'parinibbana'. There is a Brahma in Hinduism, which can replace 'the hot spring'. I won't demonstrate other religions, for those religious words actually indicate the same "place" and the same "enlightenment".

May 2017

2 The Birth of the Universe and the Truth about "Me" (The Basic In-depth Chapter)

In this part, I will use orthodox language to explain the birth of the universe and your truth, so as to lay a solid foundation for you to remove all the worries in this world. This part succeeds the beginning part of the required reading message (The Foundational Part), so you need to read it in sequence to fully understand the whole message.

First, I will make a noun explanation that will help you better understand the information of this part. Definition and differentiation of consciousness and sub-consciousness: with reference to the first part, the small water drop in the hot spring produces the intangible consciousness due to a little idea. The consciousness does not experience a sense of deprivation and guilt at birth, it does not experience fear and other feelings, either. Such a pure consciousness at that tie is called "Consciousness". After that, this pure consciousness experiences a sense of deprivation, guilt, fear and hatred, and "Consciousness" then becomes sub-consciousness, which can also be called delusional mind. This is the definition and differentiation of "Consciousness" and sub-consciousness.

In the following, I will use orthodox words to illustrate the message. First, with reference to the last part, I will elaborate on your home and the real state in which you exist in detail: in a field of awareness with no time or space, there is an eternal abstract life without beginning or end, and this life also resembles an "eternal state"; its properties are intangibility, perfection, changelessness, eternity, infinity, purity, integrity, richness, holiness, endless succession, all-embracing holy love, non-duality, and pure unity. If I use a noun to replace the word 'this life', the noun can be 'God', 'true God', or 'perfect Creator'. This life is your entire home, because the real you is only a perfect spirit created by this eternal life. And you, the perfect spirit, are created by this eternal life from within him, so you are not separated from this eternal life at the moment of your birth.

In this way, when you are created by God (eternal life), you are exactly the same as God. You are an intangible, perfect, changeless, eternal, infinite, pure, complete, rich, holy, abstract, spirit, and eternally so. You live in God, and he lives in you. Thus, at the moment you are created, you are integrated with God forever, and you are forever integrated with an infinite number of other spirits created by God. Moreover, you, the infinite number of spirits, enjoy everlastingly bliss and abundance within God forever after your birth. That's the truth about you.

However, now you've forgotten the truth completely. So how did you forget this truth? It started when God created you. After God created you, the perfect spirit would experience eternal bliss within God. But at the moment of you enjoying eternal bliss, a little circumstance arises, which is that a little idea without foundation emerges. It was similar to "what if I was to develop myself outside of God". But as this idea emerged, you as a spirit entered a state of mind wandering. Then, you lost all feelings of being in God in an instant. At the same time, with that little idea, something new appeared within you out of nowhere, which was the imageless consciousness. And the first cognition produced by this consciousness was "the feeling of bliss is gone, and I am no longer in God". This was the first "split" between you and God.

The first "split": from a state of spirituality, you follow a little idea into a state of mind wandering and produced an imageless consciousness, and mistook yourself for being out of God.

Then, two opposing speculations arose within this imageless consciousness. The first speculation was that "my separation from God is only an illusion". The second speculation was that "I'm really dissociated from the God and I can develop on my own". These two speculations pitted against each other within the consciousness and the consciousness finally accepted the second one.

This was the second "split" that reinforced the first "split": two speculations arose within the consciousness, and then consciousness accepted the second one.

Then, this imageless consciousness 'realized' that it was dissociated from God, but it did not know anything else at that time, because it only knew and remembered God. Therefore, this imageless consciousness was left alone in a state without space and time after its birth. It then continually recalled the blissful feelings of being in God, and compared those feelings with its current feelings. After the comparison, it considered that it had lost all blissful experiences and security, and this consciousness produced a great sense of deprivation. And then it had a fatal idea due to the great sense of deprivation, that is, it thought it was a big mistake to be dissociated from God's home, and by then it experienced an exceptionally great sense of guilt. It occurred to this imageless consciousness that it leaving God without notice was an absolute rebellion against him, and that it leaving without notice must make God very angry. By then, an enormous fear of being retaliated and destroyed by God had arisen within it.

In this way, after a series of thoughts, this consciousness was completely involved with guilt, compunction and fear. This consciousness became sub-consciousness at that time. At last, these huge negative feelings, especially the great fear of being destroyed by God, went beyond the ultimate limit the sub-consciousness could endure and drove it insane. Then, this insane sub-consciousness thought of escape as the only way out and immediately put it into practice. At the moment that it escaped; the following things simultaneously happened:

1. The moment the sub-consciousness escaped, it designed a completely opposite world to the home of God out of nowhere, because only such a world could enable it to forget the angry God, only such a world could serve as the final destination of the sub-consciousness. The characteristics of God's home are the unitary existence for all lives, imageless, perfect, changeless, eternal, infinite, pure, complete, rich, endlessly successive, and pure unitary. The characteristics of the world designed by sub-consciousness were the individual existence for all "lives", image, peculiarity, change, time, restraint, complexity, separation, scarcity, death, and binary opposition.

2. The sub-consciousness fantasized and projected hundreds of billions of galaxies and a nearly infinite number of separate bodies without foundation in an instant. At the same time, it expelled all guilt into these galaxies and bodies. Moreover, "projecting galaxies and bodies" and "expelling sins into them" were done simultaneously in an instant. The process can also be understood as follows: at the moment when sub-consciousness projected all guilt senses out, these guilt senses were magically transformed into a world that was diametrically opposite to the home of God. The reason why the sub-consciousness did this was because all fear was derived from guilt within it, so it had to expel guilt out if it wanted to get rid of all fear. This was the foundation of the appearance of the universe.

3. At the same time, the sub-consciousness also entered a body projected by it. This body was not different from other bodies, but the projection of the body was the most critical step for the sub-consciousness to drive guilt out. Since there was no distinction between the external and the internal for an imageless sub-consciousness, it had to use a body to differentiate the internal from the external so it could drive guilt out. So at the moment the sub-consciousness projected sins out and transformed them into the universe, it directly went into a body, so that what was inside the body became the internal and what was outside the body became the external. In this way, sins were not inside it but formed the universe outside it, thus its guilt and fear also disappeared. Furthermore, as the sub-consciousness entered a body, it gave rise to a new consciousness, that is, the self-consciousness. And the first cognition that was produced after the birth of the self-consciousness was as follows: "I am a new body, I am innocent". At this point, the self-consciousness had completely forgotten that he was once sub-consciousness, and completely forgot God's home, too.

4. The birth of the Universe revolved around a core connotation, which was the ultimate goal of the sub-consciousness. After the birth of the universe and self-consciousness, the self-consciousness forgot the sub-consciousness, but the sub-consciousness did not disappear, because at this time the sub-consciousness had just merged with the self-consciousness. That is to say, at the moment when the sub-consciousness entered a body,

it not only gave rise to the self-consciousness, but also directly merged with the self-consciousness. So why did the sub-consciousness merge with the self-consciousness? This is because the self-consciousness was bound to a body. The body had six organs: eyes, ears, nose, tongue, body and brain. These six organs corresponded to six categories in the universe: sight, hearing, smell, taste, touch and thinking. Sight could see tangible and physical objects; hearing could hear all kinds of sounds; smell could smell all kinds of smells; taste could taste all kinds of tastes; and touch could experience different body feelings. Thinking could analyze the natural laws of the universe and generate countless perceptions. For example, you know a glass would be broken if it fell on the ground, so you hold it tightly when you take it, which is a perception generated by thinking in correspondence to gravity and physics.Perceptions generated by thinking echo the natural laws of the universe all the time. So the sub-consciousness had to use a body bound to the self-consciousness to verify the reality of the universe, which is the reason why the sub-consciousness had to merge with the self-consciousness. In other words, the sub-consciousness simply transformed itself into a universe full of natural laws, and also transformed itself into the self-consciousness with a body at the same time. The sub-consciousness then used the interactions between these two aspects to confirm the authenticity of both sides. Only in this way could the sub-consciousness confirm that it had fled to a real world that was diametrically opposite to God's home. And the sub-consciousness had to stay in this state, so it constantly manipulated all the changes in the universe, and controlled the way the self-consciousness and the body saw things and thought about everything else outside the body, and it constantly manipulated the self-consciousness to recognize itself as a body. In this way, the self- consciousness and the body became the best tools for the sub-consciousness to verify the universe as real. This is the most important core connotation of the birth of the universe.

The above long exposition is the third "split" between you and God: consciousness became sub-consciousness because of great guilt and fear; from the angle of the subconscious, you projected the universe and a myriad of things of various forms and a nearly infinite number of bodies, and you also entered a body at the same time. The body was the current

The Road of Miracles

"you", and "you" lived in a third "split". Moreover, you were controlled by the sub-consciousness. Destiny in the world represents the manipulation of the sub-consciousness over you.

All the above narration is the truth about the world and you. These truths are also described in human classical works. Yet narration about the origination of the universe and Genesis in many human classical works are totally wrong. For some classical works recognize the Creator to be perfect love, while stating that perfect love (perfect Creator) created human beings and the world. If you think about it carefully, that is impossible. Even the world cannot verify such an argument. Have you ever seen a dog give birth to a camel? Have you ever seen an elephant give birth to an ant? If the Creator is the perfect love and the primal existence, how can he know anything but the perfect love, and how can he create something he does not know? If the Creator is eternal, how can he create bodies that could die and decay?

Perfect love can only produce perfect love. Perfect love must create his child after his own appearance. This is the inevitable truth. So, the world you see is not created by God (perfect love). The world was created by you alone after you, the spirit, who had mistakenly thought it had left God. So the world and all your life experiences in the world have nothing to do with God, because your God has done nothing.

I have illustrated the birth of the universe in the most orthodox language, in order to help you lay a strong foundation for learning. The followings are some common senses about the universe and life, which can also open a window for your mind.

1. First of all, I will talk about a piece of scientific common sense. It can prove that the universe is a masterpiece of sub-consciousness. Scientists have already proved that the speed of light is 300,000 kilometers per second. If the universe exploded at the same speed as the speed of light, or the universe exploded at a speed lower than the speed of light, human beings will surely see the whole picture of the universe. But human beings can't see it, which proves that the universe must explode much faster than

light, so that human beings can't see the whole picture of the universe. Scientists have proven that it is impossible for a thing to have a speed higher than that of light, to form a tangible and physical object. So, scientists cannot explain the form of the cosmic explosion, because the form of a cosmic explosion must conform to the following two points:

(1) The universe must explode at a speed much higher than that of light.

(2) It must form tangible and physical objects.

So there is only one way to satisfy these two points, that is, the projection of illusion or the imagination of mind, because only that can be faster than the speed of light and form tangible and physical object. For example, if you now imagine the sun, the image of the sun will immediately appear in your heart or mind. So thoughts are faster than anything, and they form images. Therefore, the creation of the universe is only a masterpiece created by the sub-consciousness in an instant, but the masterpiece also includes your self-consciousness and your body, so it is difficult for your self-consciousness to perceive that the universe is just a sham image. The correct description of a cosmic explosion is: Based on split, the sub-consciousness projected all the galaxies at one stroke, and instantly designed the distance and mode of operation between them.

2. Extend the above scientific common sense: the universe you see has boundaries. The universe was projected by your sub-consciousness, after you, as the perfect spirit. It mistakenly thought you had left God, and 'your' guilt and fear reached their ultimate limit, so the universe has boundaries. The reason is simple. If fear had had no limits, the universe would not have appeared. Now that the universe has already appeared, meaning that fear has limits. Thus, like fear, the universe has limits. It's just that the edge of the universe has not been seen by human beings, and beyond the tangible and physical universe is an endless void. So you just live in a limited, exceptionally big dream, and eventually you will wake up completely from this limited dreamland, because you are not a role in the dream. The dream is bound to have an end.

3. I will briefly talk about death in the world. Everyone in the world will die, which is actually a hangover from the universe's explosion. Since the sub-consciousness suffered guilt and fear of being destroyed by God before it projected the universe, sins leading to destruction became an inherent belief in the sub-consciousness. Then, after the sub-consciousness projected sins and transformed them into the universe and all beings, the belief that sins could lead to destruction pervaded within all beings and was transformed into death in the world, where only death could wipe out all sins in the world. This is the fundamental cause for the fact that all mortal beings will die. But you only die in dreams.

4. I will now briefly describe samsara. If you believe in samsara, you can read this part. If you don't believe it, you can skip this part. I have just stated that the death of the human world is only a manifestation of the sins and destruction in the sub-consciousness, that is, the sub-consciousness itself carries the death of all beings. So the death of the body can't destroy the sub-consciousness, and even the self-consciousness will not disappear because of the death of the body, because the sub-consciousness has merged with the self-consciousness, so death of the body is just an illusion for the self-consciousness and the sub-consciousness. When death comes, you just seem to be dead, because after you die, your sub-consciousness will continue to manage your self-consciousness to bind a new non-physical soul. At that time you are still controlled by the sub-consciousness. You are going to enter a baby's body again and greet a new life. This new life has no difference from the last one, because this new life is just waiting for another death. This is samsara. But as you know, you are only in samsara in dreams. No matter how many times you are in samsara, it is only a continual dream.

To sum up, you are just living in a dream controlled by the sub-consciousness, you are dreaming of space and time, dreaming that you were born on the earth, dreaming that you are a body, dreaming of your parents, dreaming of your name, dreaming of your primary school, dreaming of you marrying someone, dreaming of your life experiences, and dreaming of your death, dreaming of becoming a soul after death, and dreaming of becoming another person after the reincarnation. But most importantly, the universe has been dreamt by you alone, and there is no one else outside you, including me, the narrator that you are dreaming of. I am just reminding you now in your dream, "you are dreaming".

The above message is the last lesson of life, and the one you are destined to learn. It gives you a clear idea of who you are and the sequence in which the world came into being. This gives you the opportunity to make new choices, because you have only one power of choice in this world. From now on, you may not believe in the way your sub-consciousness appears and controls you. Starting with the next part, I will explain a few important thought patterns that are practical ways to remove all your worries, and to end this dream. These patterns will also remarkably shorten the time you wake up from your dream.

I will end with one more question that you might ask, which a lot of people are asking, "why do I, as a spirit within God's homestead, suddenly come up with a little idea? What's the reason for that?"

The answer to this question is that: there was no cause, nor consequence for that little idea that occurred to you, as a spirit within the homestead of God. Since the idea itself represents delusion, and delusion represents nonexistence and meaninglessness, no one can describe how a nonexistent and meaningless empty thought is formed, because it is nothing. So the consciousness produced along with this little thought is also illusory, and the final products generated by that consciousness, the universe and the body bound to the self-consciousness, are also utterly illusory and non-existent. So, you just living in an impossible situation. It is also a description of the world by a certain religion, called a world of ignorance, which means an illusory world created by a delusional idea without cause or consequence.

I, as a narrator, acknowledge that there are many happy things in this non-existent and fantasy world. But I can tell you the truth that these pleasures are not comparable to what the son of God really is. The joy of the world is so short, as transient as a fleeting cloud; what you own in your life is like quicksand in your hand, at the moment of death, and there is nothing left. So, you decide for yourself whether you want to continue learning the rest of the message.

My main content comes from two sets of books, called "A Course in Miracles" and "The Disappearance of the Universe" series. "The Disappearance of the Universe" is the main auxiliary textbook of "A Course in Miracles", which is easy to understand. These two sets of books are multilingual ones, which are sold in major bookstores and online stores around the world.

June 2017

Note: starting from the next part, I will use the "Kingdom of God" instead of "the home of God".

3 Forgiveness and Giving

From this part, I will use various examples in everyday life to explain a new set of thought system, and what I state in the required readings is the stress and difficulties in that thought system, but the illustration of them is enough to cover the interpretation of things happening every day in your life. So, when you have understood the stress and difficulties in the required readings, you can immediately apply them in your own life, to remove most of the worries in life, and directly change your own destiny. The ultimate goal of learning is to practice in life, without exception.

Before my illustration, firstly I will clarify two views, because these two views are the basis of practicing this thought system. These two views are as follows: 1. Why is it a thought system that can remove all the worries in the world? 2. The law of operation of sins in the world.

1. Why is it a thought system that can remove all the worries in the world?

In the previous two parts of the message, I have elaborated on the origin of you and the world, and why the sub-consciousness manipulates your self-consciousness to treat the world as real, so if you constantly recognized the world as true in thinking, you would have sustainable access to some of the most basic mental experiences, which can be summarized as satisfaction, anger, anxiety, grief and fear.

(1) Satisfaction: the sense of security that arises when your wishes and needs are met. For example, your material life has been secured, or you have an ideal relationship, all those will make you happy.

(2) Anger: attacking others because they do not meet your requirements; or fighting back because they have wronged innocent you.

(3) Anxiety: you worry that you won't get a certain relationship or some worldly fame and fortune, or worry that your future is not as good as your present situation.

(4) Grief: you feel sad for losing something you have, including the death of relatives, etc.

(5) Fear: that is dread, all kinds of fear are always following everyone. One of the most characteristic fears is that you feel guilty about something you did in the past, so you fear some retribution in the future, which upsets you.

These are some of the most basic heartfelt feelings in the world, and they are all based on your mental judgment of all the characters and events. You have never stopped mental judgment in your life, so you will be constantly experiencing those feelings in heart.

Such is the function of mental judgment. Every different mental judgment is bound to bring different heartfelt feelings, so thinking always leads the way. In the world, everyone first uses their thinking to judge everything in the world and then takes action. The purpose of this mental judgment and action is clear: to get as many "good" heartfelt feelings as possible and avoid some "bad" heartfelt feelings. This is the ability people are learning all along and the greatest pursuit for people to live in this world. However, most of what people experience in life are not "good" heartfelt feelings, and even if people have gotten some "good" heartfelt feelings, they cannot keep these experiences for a long time. You can understand it after just thinking. For example, when you were poor, you thought that you would be satisfied when you had money. But now you are rich, but are you satisfied? Or you thought that if you got married, you would be secure. But now that you are married, do you feel secure? Or, you are now the head of a big group, but are you really relaxed? The answers to these questions are self-evident.

In this world, there seems to be a defect in people's heart that can never be filled. When people get what they want and acquire the "good" heartfelt feelings, you will find these things have no value, and before long all kinds of new troubles and deficiencies come into being, then people will begin a new pursuit. In the end, this state becomes a cycle of "to seek but not find", and this endless loop is like a spell that follows you until the death. Therefore, human beings' lives can be summarized as the saying, "people will not be always be happy and flowers will not be always red; flowers can blossom after withering whereas people cannot become young again after getting aged". In the end, you can only find despair and death in this world. This is the life of everyone.

To sum up, when you think that the world really exists and you pursue in it, you are bound to get a lot of "bad" heartfelt feelings, and these "bad" heartfelt feelings are all your troubles. It can be drawn that all your troubles are built on a thought system that takes the world as real. So in order to remove all your worries, you have to change your view of the world first, and that's the purpose for which I depict in the first two parts. Because only when you understand that the world is only a dream and you are just a character in that dream, you will begin to learn and practice the other thought system recognizing the world as illusory, so you can gradually give up the thought system taking the world as real; therefore, in this process, your heartfelt feelings will directly push out all "bad" experiences, and jump straight into a spiritual experience that you have never underwent. The main attributes of this new spiritual experience is eternal peace, without opposition, and consistent. This is the reason why it is a thought system that can remove all worries. This is also the reason that thinking always leads the way.

2. The law of working of guilt in the world.

There is a law in the world; if you give something to someone else, you will lose it. For example, if you give someone a birthday present, you can buy it with money first, and then give it to someone else, then it becomes someone else's. This is true in the world. To give is to lose. But here's an example that I have to state. It will give you a deeper understanding of what this law means.

For example, you are a smoker. One day, you were smoking in the corridor of the company. It happened that one of your colleagues forgot to bring cigarettes, and then he said to you, "I forgot to bring cigarettes today. Do you have any? May I have one?". You answered, "Yes I have, please take mine". Then you pulled out your cigarettes and gave him one, which is a common scene in life.

Now let me change the situation. One day, you were smoking in the corridor of the company. Your colleague came to you without cigarettes and said, "I forgot to bring cigarettes today. Do you have any? May I have one?". You answered, "Yes I have, please take mine". And then, after you said that, you didn't do anything. At this time your colleague saw you did not give him a cigarette, and said to you, "be quick, give me one hey! What are you doing standing there?" You answered again, "Ok, Ok, you take mine". And then you just stood there and did nothing. Finally, your colleague went crazy. He said to you, "do you have any cigarettes? You stupid, just silly stand there; if you have a cigarette, give it to me! Only when you give me one can you prove you have cigarettes!" That is all this case is about.

In this case, your colleague's last words are "Only when you give me one can you prove you have cigarettes!" It means that your colleague did not believe you had cigarettes any longer, unless you gave him one to prove it. So for you, you have to give it out to prove you have it. That is to say, "what you have given proves what you have". That's how sins work in the world.

Guilt is an intangible concept. When you attack others for changing them in your life and when you hate others or cursing them for retribution, you are giving the concept of guilt away to others. You don't think it is a problem in life, because you always believe that giving sins away to others doesn't make any difference to you, but is that really the case? Absolutely not.

You can recall how you hate others in your life. When you hate others, do you have such thought: "What bad things did I do at that time? How could I have known him? If I hadn't been with him, I wouldn't be in such a situation. I really deserve it". This thought, or similar thoughts, is what happens to everyone. This is the true law of working of guilt, you cannot break away from the intangible concept of guilt because you have given it away into the others. On the contrary, when you give away the intangible concept of guilt into others through thinking, you will have both a sense of guilt and self-hatred. It is like the example that I just gave. It is only when you give a cigarette to others that can prove you have cigarettes, because you are unable to give what you do not have, so what you can give to others guarantees what you have. That is how guilt works in the world. It is in this way that sins appear out of nowhere in everyone's mind.

If you don't believe the above laws, you can do an experiment now. You can think of someone now, and if the person you think of is your best friend, you will immediately feel comfortable. If you think of an enemy, you feel uncomfortable right away. This is an evidence of the law of guilt.

Moreover,most negative feelings everyone experiences in life are derived from the process of "driving the concept of guilt out". In short, the process is that you firmly believe that you are an innocent victim, and you are victimized by the unalterable sinners (you can't change their mind and cognition) around you. This process is not only a mode of conviction, but also a kind of mental judgment that people adopt in order to achieve innocence. However, this process not only fails to lead to the acquisition of innocence, but also leads to the perception in the dark that one is a sinner and lives in a situation of being punished, which is the root of most worries in the world. This process is the same as the original pattern of the universe being projected by the sub-consciousness in order to achieve innocence. The birth of the universe is a failure of the sub-consciousness to drive guilt out in order to achieve innocence.

The above narration is the law of the working of sins in this world, and it can also be extended, "what concept you give away to others in thinking will be what you'll have and experience". It is not just the law of sins in this world and also a fixed rule for mental judgment and heartfelt feelings, because each intangible concept first will be given away through your thinking (whether to others or to yourself), then you will experience this concept in your mind. So, "the concepts you give away to others from your mind will be what you will have and experience" or the mental law that you cannot possibly transgress in the dreamed human world. This mental law always applies to everyone, with no exception.

You should ponder deeply over those above two insights, because they are the foundation upon which you can learn the other thought system. And these two insights can also show you that the most likely place to cause worries and suffering is within the interaction of human relationships. Because if there is no human interaction, people don't push the sins to and from.

Certainly, you might say, "my worries don't come from relationships". For example, you might say, "my trouble is that I can't earn more money, I can't afford a good car or house, which is not related to relationships". Well, then I ask you, "If you don't have a family, a wife, or a child, and you don't have any responsibilities, are you bothered by these?" So, much of the troubles in your life comes from the interaction of interpersonal relationships, because sometimes you don't want to take pains to live up to others' expectations. Sometimes, you worry that you will live in an undesirable situation if you can't meet other people's demands. Or, you don't want to sacrifice too much for others, because they simply ignore your efforts. So, in order to remove all your worries, you have to change your thinking pattern in the interaction of interpersonal relationships.

Here I begin with a very common life incident to illustrate the basic thinking pattern of this thought system. I will first analyze this example and then respectively bring you into the attacker side and the attacked side for illustration.

One day, you were driving your car on the road, but a car driving slowly suddenly appeared in front of you, which stood in your way. You started pressing the horn, but the car still drove very slowly. At this time, you started to get angry, and then you found an opportunity to overtake the car and opened the window to scold the driver, "Can you drive? You idiot. You drive so slowly, what about the cars behind you?" Then you closed the window and drove away. It was finished.

First of all, I will make a brief description of all your mental activities and heartfelt feelings in the event: when you were driving on the road, you needed an environment that allows you to drive fast, but you were deprived of that environment by a slow car in front of you. At this time, you had a sense of deprivation. Because you couldn't drive fast, you might not be able to catch up time, then you had a certain amount of fear. At the same time, you thought it was the driver in front of you that caused your sense of deprivation and fear, so you pushed the sins against him and started hating him, and then you attacked him. So, in the process, your self-hatred and guilt would sometimes emerge, and maybe you would think, "What immoral things have I done today? What a bad luck! I'm not happy with the slow car in front of me". These are all your mental activities and heartfelt feelings in this event.

How do these mental activities and heartfelt feelings come about? What are the disadvantages brought by these thoughts and experiences for you? I will illustrate them in detail.

Let us start with the consciousness. It is because of losing "a perfect state" that caused the consciousness to have a great deficiency, then great guilt, hatred, and fear. At that time, the consciousness became the sub-consciousness. Then, when these negative feelings went beyond the ultimate limits that the sub-consciousness can endure, the sub-consciousness projected guilt to form the universe and all living beings. And in the process, the sub-consciousness simultaneously entered a body and gave rise to the self-consciousness. So, when all had been done, the self-consciousness had forgotten the sub-consciousness, but the sub-consciousness had not let go of the self-consciousness, because at that time the self-consciousness had not only become a fundamental tool for the sub-consciousness to prove the universe true, it was also a fusion product generated by the mode of expelling sins of the sub-consciousness. So, since the birth of the self-consciousness, it not only was being controlled by the sub-consciousness, but also directly inherited the ability of expelling

26

sins from the sub-consciousness. In this way, after the birth of the self-consciousness, the sub-consciousness had continually manipulated the self-consciousness to operate under its pattern of "projecting sins". That is to say, an instinctive way of thinking for the self-consciousness in the world was to "giving away sins into other things and other bodies". That is why you were thinking like this in this case.

However, your self-consciousness had never understood that the world outside you and all the bodies and images in it were only an exceptionally big dream your sub-consciousness had fantasized, which was neither true nor false, and did not really exist, either. So, your self-consciousness couldn't really expel the sins out of your body. On the contrary, in this dreamland magically produced by the sub-consciousness, the concept you gave to others would be made out of nowhere and experienced by your mind, and the concept would remain in your sub-consciousness at the same time. This is why you had such a heartfelt feeling in this case. In terms of this instance, the driver driving slowly in front of you was just an illusory image magically produced by your sub-consciousness, and he did not exist at all. So when you gave sins to that illusion, the sins would be made out of nowhere and would be kept in your sub-consciousness at the same time.

You might think, "Well, it is nothing. I have already driven away, and I can forget about it in a minute, so it is over. There is no need to analyze it". Yes, this was the end of your personal thinking. And you could forget it in a few minutes. But this thing was far from being over for your sub-consciousness, because your sub-consciousness would not forget the sins given and owned because your mind had forgotten it.

Then, the key point is, what does this guilt kept in the sub-consciousness bring about? That is, the guilt in the sub-consciousness, because sins must trigger the guilt. The kind of guilt is divided into two categories, including one that can be perceived by your individual thinking and the other that cannot be perceived. Take this case as an example. After you scolded the slow driver, you drove away. After a while, you forgot about it. This is the situation that the guilt was not perceived by individual thinking.

However, if you scolded the slow driver, the driver opened the window and said to you, "Excuse me, I'm a new driver." So, are you still angry? At this point, you will think, "why, everyone was once a new driver, why did I scold him?" Or, the slow driver didn't respond to you at that time, and you calmed down afterwards to recall the incident, thinking that the slow driver did not know you, so he was not against you. At that time, you would have some regret. This is the situation that the guilt was perceived by your thinking. Certainly, no matter whether guilt was perceived by your thinking, sins were bound to trigger the guilt in your sub-consciousness.

Then, a more critical question arises: what did the guilt in the sub-consciousness bring about? That was punishment, for at the moment of the birth of the sub-consciousness, it firmly believed that sins and guilt were to be punished and destroyed. So, for the sub-consciousness, sins and guilt had to be removed through punishment only, so what was punishment by the sub-consciousness? In this case, you were driving on the road some day after you scolded the driver, and you were answering the phone, so you were driving very slowly and overtaken by a car while hearing a sound, "You idiot, can you drive?" This is the form of punishment for the guilt of the sub-consciousness took. Certainly, this kind of punishment may vary in form, but the content of it would never change, and you would experience the adversity of being attacked and convicted by others on a certain date, or you would experience some kind of physical injury. Because your sub-consciousness had already merged with your self-consciousness, and always believed that you were this body. So, punishment was bound to revolve around your self-consciousness and this body. This is retribution for "cause and effect" the common people often say, and it was also the correlation of sins, guilt, and punishment in the sub-consciousness.

So in this world, all the adversities and all the bad relationships that you have had in your life come from this circle of cause and effect, and sometimes you wonder why your destiny is like this. Actually, your bad fortune was caused by all your convictions and making sins in the past (sometimes the past got across transmigration). These sins led to the guilt in the sub-consciousness again and again. The guilt made all kinds of bad circumstances for you to experience, and these experiences included the pains of disease and death. That is the origin of destiny. Certainly, you also had a lot of good experiences in your life, which was because you did a lot of things benefiting others in the past (sometimes the past got across transmigration), and the things benefiting others would produce hope retained in the sub-consciousness, and then these hopes would make favorable circumstances in life for you to experience. This is why pain and pleasure goes hand in hand in one's life. This is the form and content of the saying "Receive rewards for one's virtuous deeds, evil will be recompensed with evil". You can find this form and content from people around you and yourself. I do not want to explain it. But in short, all of your life experiences are the results of the guilt and hope of the sub-consciousness.

One point needs to be stated, that how to get favorable circumstances is not what I want to illustrate. I have already made it clear that good life experiences and heartfelt feelings are not sustainable, and they are only based on bad experiences, like the saying goes that "Happiness in bitterness is still bitterness". So, what I'm going to emphasize is just to tell you how you can break away from this dreamland of "good versus bad". Then, on top of this real goal, you can get the fringe benefits: reversing bad fortune.

Then, I'm going to use this example to illustrate the use of the other thought system and the benefits it can bring to you. I will repeat the example again.

One day, when you were driving your car on the road, but a car driving slowly suddenly appeared in front of you, which stood in your way. Then, you started pressing the horn, but the car still drove very slowly. At that time, you started to get angry, and then you found an opportunity to overtake the car and opened the window to scold the driver, "Can you drive? You idiot. You drive so slowly, what about the cars behind you?" Then you closed the window and drove away.

In terms of this instance, when you were angry and experiencing a lot of negative emotions, if you could be vigilant, that is to say, if you could realize this world was just a dream generated by the sub-consciousness and realized your thoughts were manipulated by the sub-consciousness in the process of the whole incident, you could first stop thinking in accordance with the conviction mode of the sub-consciousness. You can use the other thought system to deal with this current incident, and it enabled you to think as follows: "1. The slow driver ahead of me is just an illusory image made by my sub-consciousness. He doesn't really exist. The incident of his car blocking my way is just a part of my dream. So, I don't have to hate and attack the driver ahead of me. Because if I convicted him, the guilt would be in my sub-consciousness and bring a lot of negative feelings to me. 2. The true identity of the driver ahead of me is just a spirit in the kingdom of God. He is within the same God together with me. He and I have never left God and are pure without guilt". Such thinking modes are the two basic thinking modes in this new thought system of thinking, called true forgiveness thinking and giving innocence.

When you practice these two thinking modes based on the above event, you will not attack the driver again, because when you practice true forgiveness, the driver ahead of you will become an illusion and lose meaning and the world will also become an illusion and lose meaning. Then, you as the subject (your body and body-bound self-consciousness) will become an illusion along with everything outside of you and the meaning of it will be undone. Then the sub-consciousness that is magically transformed into you and the world will lose its meaning, too. Then your mind will be completely free from the control of the sub-consciousness. Then, you give innocence to others, and innocence will be immediately experienced by you. At that time, your mind will jump out of the negative experiences that all conviction modes generate, and will jump into a brand new spiritual experience that is an eternal peace without opposition. One of your troubles will have been removed. And when you practice true forgiveness and give innocence, you will not make a new sin. If there is no new sin, there will be no new guilt. You will not experience the situation of new punishment in the future. Then your destiny has been changed. That is the fringe benefit you will get.

To sum up, the idea of true forgiveness is to realize that the person or event in front of you is a dream, and to give innocence is to bestow the idea of innocence into someone or some people. The combination of these two thoughts not only enables you to get out of all negative feelings, but also enables you to find your innocence. It is like a conviction. It is at that time that you first remove the meaning of the whole illusory world and the self-consciousness from your mind, to give the idea of innocence to others. You will not only have the innocence, but also directly become innocence, because everything in the world has been forgiven by you, and only the innocence you have given remains. So, with true forgiveness, you become what you have given. The sign of your becoming innocence is that your mind experiences eternal peace. And this kind of peace can only be experienced through your own practice.

I remind you that the practice of true forgiveness and giving innocence can be postponed for beginners, because they find it difficult to immediately apply the two thoughts to similar situations. In the case of the car driving, if you were not vigilant when you were angry, you simply scolded the driver and drove away, then when you came home and calmed down, if you could be vigilant at that time, and then practiced the above two kinds of thinking modes (for that incident) is completely viable, because this kind of postponed practice can also melt away most of the sins you gave just now, and your mind could instantly experience the eternal peace. This kind of postponed practice is absolutely beneficial, and it is also the only way which must be passed for beginners.

I'm going to bring you into the role of being attacked to illustrate, because you are in the role of being attacked many times in life, but before I explain that, I'm going to start with analyzing what the concept of 'counter-attack after you've been attacked' is.

One day you were driving on the road and answering a phone, so you were driving very slowly. Just then, a car behind you overtook you and a voice came out of the car, "You idiot, can you drive?" When you heard someone scold you, you got angry, and cursed back, "Are you going to a funeral by driving so fast? Did I provoke you?" The instance was finished.

First, I will analyze the psychological process of the counter-attack side. When you were driving, you needed an environment free of distractions, but suddenly a driver was scolding you. Not only did you lose an undisturbed environment, but also suffered attack and conviction. At that time, your sense of deprivation, anger, and hatred emerged simultaneously, and you took action to counter-attack. In the process, your mind would not only experience a lot of negative feelings, but sometimes you would experience self-hatred, and you may think, "What an unlucky life I have! I was just driving my car and got cursed by others". These are the mental activities and heartfelt feelings of counter-attack.

From the above analysis, we can see that there is no way to attack back, because when you counter-attack others, you still deal with the problem according to the conviction mode, then you would still make new sins, and the sins would still generate new guilt and new punishment circumstances for you to experience. So, if you could suddenly wake up to realize this circumstance to be an illusory one displayed by an previous sin in your sub-consciousness, then you can deal with this event by applying true forgiveness and giving innocence.

You should think of it in this way, "1. The scene in which I am attacked and convicted by a driver is just an illusory scene displayed by some previous guilt in my sub-consciousness. The scene is just a dream that does not exist. The driver who is scolding me is just an imaginary figure made by my sub-consciousness. He does not exist, so I will not fight back against him. 2. I shall look beyond his imaginary figure to see his true nature, which is a spirit in the kingdom of God, and is with me within the same God; he is guiltless and innocent; he and I have not left the kingdom of God at all". When you think and act like this, not only can you break away from the control of the sub-consciousness and acquire peace of mind, you can also defuse the previous sin in the sub-consciousness, because a punishing circumstance of being attacked and convicted which is manifested by a previous sin has been forgiven and dissolved by you, so the previous sin will disappear from your sub-consciousness. Besides, this time you do not convict someone again, so you won't have to suffer some new punishing circumstances in the future. However, it should be noted that even if you are going to experience similar circumstances of being attacked in the future, they are only generated by other previous sins in your sub-consciousness. So, you don't have to be perplexed, when you have forgiven a previous sin, that sin disappears forever.

The application of the above thinking can also be delayed for beginners. For example, if you drove away after you fought back, and then another day you turned to realize that you didn't apply true forgiveness and give innocence yesterday, then it is completely viable to practice (for yesterday's event), because it can defuse most of the sins you've given.

It is hard for beginners to feel comfortable when using these two modes of thinking in your life for the first few times, because you are already used to taking the world as real and convicting others, then it is very difficult for you to reverse this ingrained wrong mode. But you have to practice it, because it is the only way you wake up from your big human dream. If you think the world can be accepted, and you are willing to spend a few more decades or lifetimes in this dreamland, that is fine. But when you can't relish the dream any more, you will naturally and seriously study and practice this thought system out of the dream.

At the end of this illustration, I conclude with the most basic model of true forgiveness in "The Disappearance of the Universe":

You don't really exist there,
You're just the image I make,
If I convict you and see you as the cause of my problems,
Then, the guilt and fear that I hold must exist in me.
Since God and I have never been separated,
I should have forgiven something that both of us do not actually do,
And here is nothing but innocence.
I have joined with the holy spirit in peace.

In the next part, I will first outline the level of spiritual experience and the connotation of the theological word "holy spirit". This illustration will enable you to understand the general steps of awakening from the big dreams of life. Then, I'll go on to show other modes of thinking in this new thought system by using common examples of life.

Finally, several points should be stated:

1. The mode of thinking about true forgiveness and giving innocence demonstrated here is not fully applicable to the field of human work and law, especially the field of law. There is a set of independent rules in the field of work and law. In the following, I will illustrate how the field of work and law is connected with this thought system.

2. Your body won't disappear by practicing the thought of true forgiveness. Because this mode of thinking is only for your mind and your sub-consciousness, but not for your body.

3. The Thinking mode of true forgiveness only has one connotation which is different from other thinking modes. In this case, if you think in the following way without attacking someone, "I don't want to make a fuss with him. I'm not angry. There is no need for me to talk with such a low quality driver". This kind of thinking is not really true forgiveness thinking, because its connotation is still the giving and possession of sins. So you should note that there is only one kind of the connotation of true forgiveness.

4. The thinking mode of true forgiveness is a simple explanation that is intended to lay the foundation for all the later parts that will be illustrated, so if you want to learn more about all the connotations of true forgiveness, you can refer to "The Disappearance of the Universe" series by yourself.

July 2017

4 Demand and Entrustment, first half

In this part, I will first outline the levels of spiritual experience and the connotation of the theological word "holy spirit". This illustration will enable you to understand the general steps of awakening from the big dream of life. Then, I'll go on to illustrate other modes of thinking in this thought system by using the common examples of life.

First of all, I will talk about three levels of spiritual experience:

1. Experience of you as the son of God living in the kingdom of heaven. The specific feeling is as follows: you will eternally confirm that you are a spirit living within God forever, because in the kingdom of heaven, you will have an eternal feeling that you are just a completely safe, pure, innocent, bright, infinite, constant, perfect, holy, intangible, joyful, free and abstract spirit. You will be eternally certain that you are inseparable with other infinite number of spirits. This "awareness" of living within the kingdom of God is the first level of spiritual experience you can have. And only this level of experience really exists; that is to say, only the kingdom of God exists.

2. All heartfelt feelings that take the world as real, and consider yourself to be living in it in the form of a body. You can take the above part as reference to understand it. If you are also a believer in transmigration, you can add that you take the soul world after death as real and consider yourself to be living in it as a soul. These two heartfelt feelings are the second level of spiritual experiences you can have. And before you return to the kingdom of God, you can only go through these two illusory worlds of life and death, so these two worlds of life and death belong to one dream, not two.

3. The spiritual experience for practicing the thought system based on true forgiveness and giving innocence. The main attributes of this kind of spiritual experiences is a kind of eternal peace, which is without

35

opposition and consistent. This is the third level of spiritual experience you can achieve. And at this level, you can further see the illusory nature of all beings in one person from the outside, and then you can further extend the innocence from within one person outside of you into all sentient beings. At that time, you and all sentient beings will become a peaceful and abstract unitary state of mind. This state of mind can not only dissolve all heartfelt feelings that take all the illusory world as real, but also extremely resembles the kingdom of God, where you and other spirits are peaceful and in unitary existence. Therefore, this peaceful and abstract unitary state of mind can be regarded as a miraculous state of mind as compared to the second level of spiritual experience. (The miraculous state of mind is hereinafter referred to as miracle mind).

What is the origin and content of the miracle mind, and what benefits can it bring to you? So that is the key point of my analysis. In this analysis, I will also illustrate the relationship between the miracle mind and awakening and the connotations of the term "Holy Spirit".

The origin and meaning of miracle mind: when you, the spirit from the Kingdom of God was distracted by a little thought, you mistook yourself for leaving God, and projected a universe and lived in it with a series of wrong thoughts. However, this series of changes and results were basically nothing more than a dream that you, the heavenly spirit dreamt of in heaven. So, a series of changes and results did not exist and were meaningless for the kingdom of God, and your spiritual dream was also impossible to appear in the kingdom of God, so when you entered the dream, your God did not acknowledge the content of your dream, but God knew that you had entered a dream of "being lost" in which you were not feeling well. So, your God put a "voice" of awakening into you at the very moment of you falling into a dream, and this "voice" was called "the Holy Spirit". How would the Holy Spirit awaken you? What did he do within you? That is what I am going to focus on.

It started with the moment you entered the dream. When you entered the dreamland, the Holy Spirit followed you into it. But at some point, the Holy Spirit was absolutely different from you in dream. The Holy Spirit knew what was illusory and what was real, because the Holy Spirit came from God. So, the moment you projected the world, the Holy Spirit within you immediately forgave the illusory world and all sentient beings you projected, and he also gave the concept of innocence to all sentient beings. Thus, the miracle mind, the peaceful and abstract unitary state of mind, was first created by the Holy Spirit. The Holy Spirit then waited for you to follow his mode of thought, so that your mind would be reconciled with the miracle mind. So why did the Holy Spirit do this? Because if your mind was reconciled with the miracle mind for a long time, your mind would be chronically "close to" the state of the spirit living in the Kingdom of God. And this kind of long-term "closeness" would generate "qualitative change" after some time, and this "qualitative change" meant that God would pull your mind back into him at some moment, and then your mind would instantly be transformed into a spirit. When that happened, you would wake up from your dream of human life. Not only would you recognize that you were a spirit living in God, but also you would recognize that the world in front of you was a fantasized bubble that did not exist. This is the main benefit that the miracle mind can bring to you: awakening to your truth. Certainly, awakening is just a short-time experience of spiritual transformation, so your body is not going to disappear due to awakening.

In addition to this main benefit, miracle mind will bring you two side benefits.

1. Miracle mind can change destiny. In the previous part I stated that, the guilt in your sub-consciousness would manifest the adversities for you to experience, and hopes in your sub-consciousness would manifest favorable circumstances for you to experience, but the peaceful miracle mind does not belong to guilt in the sub-consciousness or hopes in the sub-consciousness, because you acquire the miracle mind through true forgiveness and giving innocence as foundation, so the first fringe benefit that this kind of mind can bring to you is as follows: miracle mind manifests a new peaceful circumstance for you to experience, and this brand new peaceful circumstance can directly replace the circumstance that the sub-consciousness has designed for you. To specify, when you practice this new thought system in the process of experiencing a life scene

and get a miracle mind, the miracle mind will immediately or gradually manifest a new peaceful circumstance for you to experience. At the same time, the adversities that your sub-consciousness has already designed for you will immediately or gradually disappear. Then your destiny has been changed. And after you have experienced this peaceful circumstance, you will not only be deeply aware that you have evaded some adversity, and you will also be surprised that this peaceful circumstance brings you such an unexpected ending to the satisfaction to everybody concerned, which alone can be called a miracle.

2. The miracle mind can shorten the time you spend in wandering in the dream. Because no new guilt or hopes will appear in your sub-consciousness as you practice this new thought system and attain this miracle mind. Without new guilt and hope, your sub-consciousness will not design new life scenes for you to experience, which will prompt the moment of awakening to come sooner. But this is illustrated from a broad sense. Originally, you should go through five times' transmigration before awakening, but because you practice this system of thoughts in this life, some of your future life scenes will disappear completely. Then, some future time will disappear together with those scenes; that is to say, you don't need more time to experience the life scenes that have disappeared, and this will shorten the time of awakening by a few lifetimes.

The information narrated above is the inner connection between the level of spiritual experience and awakening. And this information also explains the general meaning of my main textbook, "A Course in Miracles": you will get the miracle mind by practicing the mode of thinking described in this course. The primary benefit that this state of mind can bring to you is awakening to your own truth, and the fringe benefit is that it can manifest a peaceful situation for you to experience and shorten the time you spend in wandering in dream.

Hereafter I begin to explain other modes of thinking in this thought system with real life cases, and then I will narrate a real case of myself, because this real case can help you understand all the connotations of the miracle mind and peaceful situation more clearly.

In the previous part, I used a very simple driving example to describe two basic thinking patterns. It is difficult to tell all the other thinking patterns in the case of driving, so this time I will use another life example to explain. The example is as follows:

There was a family of two people, a husband and wife who were both salary workers. One day, the husband became infatuated with online games. He played games after coming back home every day. This made his wife upset. Then a few days later, the wife could not stand it any longer, and scolded her husband when he started played games, "You just play games every day, and completely ignore me. If you continue to play, you go live with the people in game! You, turn it off now!" When the husband heard this, he got angry and answered, "What's wrong with me playing games after work? Leave me alone and don't make trouble". The case was finished.

In this case, there are only two roles, one attacker and one counter-attacker. These are the two roles you often play in your life.

First, I will analyze the attacker's thinking and heartfelt feelings:

1. The wife in the case once had a husband who could accompany her every day. Because her husband was infatuated with online games, the husband that could accompany her disappeared. At that moment, there was a certain sense of deprivation in her heart.

2. On the basis of this sense of deprivation, this wife had a certain fear, because she was worried that she would live in a neglected situation for a long time if her husband kept being obsessed with online games.

3. The wife also thought that her sense of deprivation and fear were caused by her husband, so she had resentment against her husband.

4. This fear and resentment were repeated and amplified by her husband's continual playing. Finally, when fear and resentment reached the ultimate limit, the wife got angry, and she attacked her husband and asked him to change into the one who could accompany her.

Those are the complete set of a sense of deprivation, fear, conviction, anger, and thinking of changing others and heartfelt feelings of the attacker. Certainly, the wife experiences self-hatred. Because this wife sometimes also thinks, "what was wrong with me at that time, how could I marry him, now I regret so much". This is the situation that sins are directed at both her and others.

From the above analysis, we can see that when the wife was hating her husband and attacked him, she would not only experience many negative heartfelt feelings, but also made new sins in her sub-consciousness, and then new sins would fermented a new sense of guilt and new circumstances of being punished for her to experience. But in intimate relationships, the circumstances of being punished often happen immediately. This is similar to the situation in this case, when the wife convicted her husband and requested him to correct himself, her husband immediately attacked her and also asked her to change. This is the immediate manifestation of the circumstance of being punished. It is also the norm of people attacking each other in their lives: both sides continually convict each other and demand change, but both sides think the other's demands are wrong.

After analyzing the attacker, I will analyze the party of counter-attacker.

1. In this case, the husband used to have a wife who allowed him to play games, and he thought playing games would brought him a sense of satisfaction. However, that day his wife's attack on him made him realize that the wife who allowed him to play games disappeared, and at that time he had a sense of deprivation.

2. On the basis of the sense of deprivation, he had two kinds of fears: (1) he was worried that he would not be able to enjoy the satisfaction of playing games in the future. (2) He was afraid that he would become a hen-pecked husband and lose his freedom if he obeyed his wife's demands.

3. Based on his sense of deprivation and fear, the husband also received the guilt his wife assigned him, which led to his resentment and victimhood, because he always believed that playing games after work was the right thing to do.

4. These feelings of deficiency, fear, resentment, and victimhood turned to anger in an instant, and the expression of that anger usually began with an innocent face presented in front of the other person, and then fought back. So this is the situation in the case. The husband's intention to fight back was clear: he wanted his wife to be someone who gave him freedom and allowed him to play games.

These are the counter-attacker's set of deficiencies, fear, victim's emotions, conviction, anger, and thinking of changing others and heartfelt feelings.

After analyzing the mental and spiritual experiences of both parties, you can see a result that both parties have experienced a lot of negative heartfelt feelings and bad situations in this case, which is the result of people being manipulated by the sub-consciousness and living under the conviction mode.

So if you are one of the two roles in the case, what can you do to evade the manipulation of the sub-consciousness? This requires you to practice the thinking of true forgiveness and giving innocence in conjunction with the other two modes of thinking: (letting go and satisfying) demand and entrustment. I will respectively put you into the role of the attacking side and the role of the counter-attacking side for illustration.

First of all, I'm going to put you in the role of wife, and if you are the wife in this case, what are you going to do with your husband's habit of playing online games?

First, it is still vigilance, which means that if you can suddenly realize that you are manipulated by your sub-consciousness in the course of deficiency, fear, resentment again, and that you again take the image and the dream in front of you as real. Then you can stop thinking according to the manipulation of the sub-consciousness, and then you can practice the thinking pattern of true forgiveness and giving innocence; you should think, "the husband in front of me who is playing games is the image made by my sub-consciousness, and only a role in my dream; that his playing online games is an event in my dream. So I don't hate this imaginary image in front of me. The true face of my husband is a spirit in heaven. He is within the same God just as I am. He is guiltless and innocent. He and I have never left the kingdom of God. When you practice in this way, you and your husband will become a peaceful and abstract unitary state of mind: miracle mind.

Then, you need to move on to practice another thinking pattern: letting go of demands. Think about it in this way, "If I need a husband to accompany me and fill my sense of deficiency, this dreamland will redisplay some real meaning to me. That way I'm still being controlled by my sub-consciousness, so I shall choose to let go of that demand". When you think like this without action, the sense of deficiency in your heart will disappear.

Why should you practice letting go of demands? That's because your self-consciousness has been used to a fixed pattern of "pursuing something or a relationship in the world because of deficiency". The problem is that this pattern is a hoax because it directly guarantees the authenticity of deficiency. That is to say, when you are pursuing something due to deficiency, you have already defined your deficiency as true. However, if you have defined your internal deficiency as true, you can no longer satisfy it. Because everything in this world is just an illusory product of the original sense of deprivation after you mistakenly thought that you had left God; that is to say, the original deficiency was not separated from everything in the world. So, you can't rely on these illusory products to dissolve that primordial deficiency. This is why you always feel the sense of deprivation whoever you are, no matter how many materials or interpersonal relationships you have, and this is why you "seek but not find". So if you want to dissolve the sense of deficiency in your heart, you first need to understand in thinking of unity and unreality of deficiency, the self and the world, so that you can use the thought of true forgiveness and letting go of demands to dissolve it.

Fundamentally speaking, to practice letting go of demands is the imperative way out of your dream. But I'm not asking you to let go of materials and relationships you have right now. I mean that you just need to understand their illusory nature; because that is the only way you will not be bound by these illusory things.

After you practice letting go of demands, you may be able to dissolve the sense of deficiency, but the continual fear that it brings you may still remain in your mind. This fear is that you worry your husband will play games unscrupulously every day if you let him play games, which will make your chronically live in a snubbed situation. This is a persistent residual brought by your sense of deficiency. So how do you deal with this continual fear?

Think about it in this way: "if I get snubbed every day by my husband in the future, I accept it, I accept it. Because all the future situations and all the behaviors of my husband are just a dream presented by my sub-consciousness; in the future, no matter how much he is addicted to the Internet, no matter how much he snubs me, I cannot be a victim, and I will always choose to forgive and let go of demands". When you think like this, your fear of the future will disappear. So why do you think that way?

That is because the law of working of fear in the world is as follows: the more you fear that you will experience a situation in the future, the more real that situation will become in your sub-consciousness, and then it will be manifested into your life. This is the result of the fact that the whole world works within your sub-consciousness, which is also the form and connotation of "what you are afraid of will occur", a common saying.

So if you want to break away from the restraint of the law of fear, what you have to do is to reverse your thinking to confront fear at the moment of fear. The solution is to tell yourself at the moment of fear, "even if some adversity that I fear happens in the future, I accept it. I accept it. Let it be! Because none of these circumstances are real, I am not a victim even if I experience these adversities. And I haven't left the kingdom of God at all". That is the main way to break away from fear, and its connotation is to apply the thinking of true forgiveness at the moment of fear to confront some future adversity. After you have practiced this way, some future adversity will increasingly fade away in your sub-consciousness, so the situation is increasingly unlikely to be experienced by you. Even if you do encounter some adversity after confronting it, your practice won't be in vain, because it can dramatically reduce the difficulty and complexity of an adversity (within your sub-consciousness). So when this adversity does happen, you will find that it is much less difficult, and you will be able to face it leisurely. So the thought pattern of facing fear directly is an important assistance of changing your destiny.

The thoughts above about facing fear directly can be further developed. In this case, if, in addition to your fear that your husband will be playing games every day, you have another fear. For example, you are afraid that your husband's health will be affected by playing games, or that your husband's work will be affected by playing games. What can you do about it? Actually the method is the same. You think of all things you fear again at the moment of the fear, and then tell yourself, "even if all the adversities I don't want to go through happen in the future, I will accept and experience them one by one, because none of these adversities really exist. All your fears will be dissolved at that time.

To sum up, the basis of fear was taking some situation in the future seriously, and the thinking of taking some circumstance real would be controlled by the sub-consciousness. This kind of control would make you perform some mistaken mental judgments and actions at the moment of fear. At last, those mental judgments and actions would lose you in desperation of interpersonal relationships of mutual attack. That is the biggest disadvantage of fear. If you don't believe it, you can now recall the kind of mentality you have before attacking and hating people.

So, the practice of facing fear directly is the most critical step for you to achieve peace of mind. This is the second mode of thinking narrated in this part, called entrustment of fear, which is simplified as 'entrustment'. This word represents a situation where you can entrust your fear to the thinking of true forgiveness.

Finally, the thought of entrusting fear has an important role, that is, it can prevent you from evading and forgetting the fear. For example, people often think at the moment of fear, "I'm bored to death. I can't think about this anymore. I can't stand it. I will deal with it later". This is a common trick people use to evade and forget about their fears, but it is a futile one for dissolving fear, because it just shelves them in the sub-consciousness. So, you should stop evading and forgetting about fear, and why you are chased by them. In fact, you who are physically and mentally exhausted just needs to face all that you fear directly and then you will find that what you fear is nothing.

These are all the modes of thinking that you need to practice as a wife. After you have finished practicing these modes of thinking, peace will enter your fearless mind. Your husband and you will be firmly united in the miracle mind of peace. Your miracle mind will bestow you an inspiration to do the right thing, which will let you know that you don't have to do anything. At that time, you don't have to stop your husband from playing with the computer, nor attack your husband. Then, this miracle mind will immediately or gradually manifest a peaceful circumstance and outcome for you to experience. This case is just a case for me to explain, so I can only give a rough idea of this peaceful situation. Your husband will probably give up online games over time and accompany you more. And you will find that you have gained some benefits and evaded some misfortune after you have experienced the whole peaceful situation. But temporarily I'm not going to use this example to tell you what benefits you will gain and what adversities you will evade. Because I will use a real case of mine to make a targeted explanation, as you can see in the second part.

The practice of the thinking modes above can be postponed for beginners. If you have already quarreled with your husband, it's completely viable to be vigilant and practice all these thinking modes. Or it can be procrastinated for later.

Finally, two points to be stated:

1. The entrustment of fear narrated in this part is not completely applicable to the workplace in the world. Because the rules of the workplace are all about respective responsibilities, clear demarcation of right and

wrong, proper reward and punishment. So, if you fail in your job or make a mistake, you are very likely to be punished or fired even if you consign your fear.

2. All the modes of thinking narrated in this part are not applicable to the legal category of the world. The laws of the world are basically fixed rules of restraining the body made by your sub-consciousness. So, the mode of thinking is not beyond the laws of the world. If you do something that violates the law, you will be punished by the law, and put in jail. But the laws of the world bind only the body, but not the mind.

That is the end of the first half. In the second half, I will explain the method as if you played the role of husband.

August 2017

5 Demand and Entrustment, second half

Let us make a simple review of heartfelt feelings and the situation of the party attacked. In the case, the husband was playing games and suddenly received his wife's attacks and a request for his alteration, which made him experience a sense of deprivation, fear and the victimhood in an instant, and then the husband counter-attacked his wife with a request to make the wife change. This is the normal process of life in which the attacked party fights back against the other, and this process is the result of the attacked party being manipulated by the sub-consciousness and living in the conviction mode.

If you are the husband in this case, how do you deal with this incident and break away from the control of the sub-consciousness? First of all, vigilance, which means if you can suddenly realize that you are being manipulated by your sub-consciousness, and again taking an image in front of you and a dream as real when you are having an argument with your wife, you can stop thinking according to the manipulation of the sub-consciousness, and practice the thinking of true forgiveness and giving innocence; you should think like this, "My wife that attacked me is an image made by my sub-consciousness. She is just a role in my dream and her attack is an event in my dream, so I won't hate this illusory image. The true nature of my wife is a spirit in heaven, within the same God with me. She is guiltless and innocent, and she and I have never left the kingdom of God". When you practice like this, your wife and you will be a peaceful miracle mind.

Then, you should continue to practice the thinking mode of letting go of demands: "1. my wife asking me to stop playing games is just a reminder that I am taking too seriously the satisfaction that playing games brings, which means that my addiction for playing games represents a kind of deficiency. So I am going to give up playing games and forgive the sense of deficiency. 2. If I need a wife who will let me play games, my sense of deficiency will become real, so I will not ask my wife to change into someone who will let me play games". When you think like this and stop playing games, the sense of deficiency in your heart will disappear.

Finally, you should practice entrusting the fear to dissolve it: "if in the future my wife meddles with me every day and doesn't let me do some things in the future, I will accept it, I will accept it. Because all circumstances in the future do not really exist, I will always choose to forgive and give up some of my demands". After you have entrusted like that, your fear of becoming a hen-pecked husband will disappear.

But this time because you are the party attacked and requested, when you complete the above practice and become the miracle mind, the peace inside you will be extended to your wife, then the peace will bring this perception to your wife: "my husband really has changed, he doesn't care to play games, and it seems that playing games do not mean anything to him. I worried too much". Up to now, your wife's fear of your becoming addicted to the internet will be replaced by this perception of peace. Your wife will not continue to attack you. Moreover, in the future, your wife will be unlikely to stop you from playing games, and then you can continue to play your games without being bound by the games. This is what a peaceful situation a miracle mind can bring you.

However, in this case, the wife's other request was involved, that she wished her husband to accompany her, and at this time the husband was in a more complicated situation. Simply speaking, the situation was: as the attacked party, when others attack you, you will be asked to let go of something yet do something else. How do you respond to such a situation? This is the key point of this part. I will extend the example of the quarrel between the young couple to explain.

There was a family of two people, a husband and wife who were both salary workers. One day, the husband became infatuated with online games. He played games after coming home every day. This made his wife upset. Then after a few days, this wife could no longer bear it, and scolded his husband when he was playing games: "you just play games every day and ignore me; you just go to live with the person in the game if you continue playing it! Turn it off now!" When the husband heard this, he got angry and answered, "What's wrong with me playing games after work? Leave me alone and don't make trouble". Then, the wife got madder and said, "How long has it been since you went shopping with me? Accompany me shopping now. If you go on playing, I will smash the computer." Then the husband continued to fight back, "Ok, smash it. I will not go". So the young couple began to quarrel with each other. It was finished.

To begin with, two points of the case will be analyzed:

1. The wife in the case took some aggressive actions because of long-term sense of deprivation and fear. Her intention was clear that she wanted her husband to give up playing games and accompany her to go shopping. Only in this way could the deficiency within her be made up. So basically speaking, her attack was just a hope that her husband can help her make up her deficiency, and her request was just a sincere voice for help.

2. The husband in the case also understood in the quarrel process that the purpose of his wife's attack was the hope that he could accompany his wife to go shopping. His situation then became the more complex situation just described: as an attacked party, someone will tell you to let go of one thing while asking you to do something else. But for this husband, why did he experience this situation of being attacked and requested while playing the computer alone?

This is because people did many things to convict others for the sense of deprivation and fear and ask them to change in the past (sometimes across reincarnations) (the analysis of the first point). The essence of these things is to ask others to make up for his deficiency. This is the habitual pattern of the thought system that "takes the world as real" to eliminate deficiency. However, this pattern won't dissolve any deficiency, because this mode and the "expelling and owning of sins" share the same mechanism: when you regard your sense of deprivation as real and ask others to make up for it, this sense of deprivation has already been driven out from you; at that time, the sense of deprivation will be retained within your sub-consciousness (whether the deficiency will be made up or not). This sense of deprivation will bide time to be manifested into a convicted and requested situation for you to experience. This is the law of the working of deficiency in the world. This is also the reason that the husband in this case went through such a situation. Therefore, for this husband, the deficiency of his wife was just a former deficiency in his sub-consciousness, and the situation he was attacked and requested was just the scene of life manifested by this former deficiency.

So, if you are the husband in this case, you need to practice the thinking of true forgiveness, giving innocence, letting go of demands and entrustment, and also practice the thought of satisfying someone's genuine demands to overcome this previous sense of deprivation. This kind of mental practice firstly requires your reverse thinking: if you do not satisfy your wife's sincere request for help, what will be the situation:

(1) If I don't want to spend illusory time and illusory energy to accompany my wife to go shopping, it proves that these illusory things still have some meaning for me.

(2) If I resist the occurrence of the shopping situation, it will prove that I have decided that going shopping with my wife will make me a kind of victim.

(3) If I think my wife's asking for help is wrong, I will probably convict my wife.

(4) My wife's sincere demand for my help is just a manifestation of a previous sense of deprivation in my sub-consciousness, so if I don't respond to her request for help, the previous deficiency will be shelved in my sub-consciousness, then the deficiency will still wait to be manifested into another situation for me to experience.

When you have done all the above converse thinking, the result is clear: if you don't respond to your wife's demand, you are more likely to be lost in dream and be manipulated by your sub-consciousness. So when you face genuine call for help from others, you can use the following positive thinking:

(1) I will put illusory time and illusory energy to satisfy my wife's sense of deficiency, because such actions indicate that I will not give any significance to these illusory objects.

(2) I don't think shopping with my wife will make me a victim, because I haven't left the kingdom of God and the victim does not exist.

(3) My wife is only a spirit in the kingdom of God, so she is innocent and free from deficiency.

(4) My wife's sincere request for help is just a manifestation of a previous deficiency in my sub-consciousness, so I am willing to experience and accept this illusory situation (shopping with my wife) to dissolve that previous deficiency.

When you have practiced these thoughts and took action, you and your wife will be firmly united in a peaceful miracle mind. Because you were the party that was asked for help, your inner peace could extend to the heart of your wife after you answered her. And that peace would give your wife the feeling, "my husband won't ignore me. It is useless worrying. I am so happy." At this time, your wife's deficiency will disappear, and this sense of deficiency will also be out of your sub-consciousness.

This is what I am talking about in this part: the thinking patter to satisfy needs (to satisfy others' genuine request of help). This thinking pattern also applies to the situation in which someone asks you to do something without attacking you. The connotation of such thinking pattern is: you need to use "action" to satisfy others' genuine request for help. And you should understand that these "actions" are illusory before you "act", so that you can "act" willingly. This is the main way to dissolve previous deficiency in the sub-consciousness.

A beginner is not required to fulfill the thinking pattern of satisfying others' genuine request for help, because the specific things that happen

51

in life can sometimes be quite complicated. So the beginner is not immediately able to distinguish which requests are the manifestation of previous deficiency and which ones are not,. The beginner is not suddenly able to recognize that the attack and request from others is only a voice for help. So, as a beginner, you can start with the little things you do in life, and then as the practice goes on, you will find more and more important and accurate methods to respond to people's genuine requests for help. This is also the normal process of practicing this thinking pattern. You shall bear in mind that everyone's sincere request for help to you is for your release from sufferings. So the hand you lend others seems to help others, but in essence, it helps yourself.

One last question you might ask is, "if I satisfy all the genuine help from others, I will lose a lot of things, including my time, energy, and money, etc. What can I gain after losing these things?" The answer is also a peaceful situation. Here is a real case of my own about what a peaceful situation is like after meeting others' sincere call for help and achieving miracle mind. In this way you can fully appreciate the benefits of these thought patterns for you.

First of all, I will list the characters: I, my wife, my one-and-a-half-year-old daughter, my mother-in-law, and a friend of mine: a doctor of traditional Chinese medicine.

Date: March 2014

Relationship: the adults in my family will go to see the doctor of traditional Chinese medicine if they are sick.

Then I will introduce one little incident before the event: a few days before I acquiring the peaceful situation, my wife had a small disease, and then she went to see the doctor of traditional Chinese medicine. The doctor of traditional Chinese medicine prescribed medicines (the prescription has more than 10 kinds of the Chinese herbal medicine), but when my wife went to the pharmacy store to buy those medicines, the pharmacist said there were two Chinese herbal medicines out of stock. The prescription was not completed, so my wife did not get this set of traditional Chinese medicine.

I will start by telling the whole event: one day in March 2014, I came back home from work at 5:30 p.m. and started eating dinner while my child was sleeping. (My child had a meal earlier that day, and it was probably over 4 o'clock. They ate noodles. After that, the child went to bed.) That's when it started. During my dinner, my mother-in-law told me that she wanted to see the doctor because she had been suffering from a cold and had an upset stomach. I said ok and I would drive you to the doctor in a minute. Then I said to my wife, "Stay at home and take care of the baby. She has not woken up." However, when my wife heard this, she told me that she was going with us, and taking the child.

When I heard this, I started to resist it, because I thought so in my heart. The weather was very cold (It is very cold during March in Tianjin), and it took 40 minutes to drive to the doctor's home, so I thought it was very inconvenient to take the child with us, and it might cause the child catch a cold. So when I finished my evaluation, I said to my wife, "the baby hasn't woken up yet. If she wakes up, we cannot take her. How do we do if the baby catches a cold?" But my wife didn't take my advice. She said she was going to wake up the baby now and took her with us. My wife thought it was no fun for her to be at home with the kid, so she wanted to take her for some fun. As a result of our disagreement, my wife and I began to quarrel.

Then, my mother-in-law saw us arguing and said, "I'm not going. I stay at home to take care of the child". My mother-in-law meant that my wife and I go to the doctor together and get a prescription from the doctor so we could avoid quarrel. But even with my mother-in-law's compromise, my wife still refused, and insisted in taking the baby with her.

In the process of the stalemate, I became vigilant, and then I began to practice all the thinking patterns shown in this part. First of all, I forgave my family members and gave them innocence. Then I practiced the act of letting go of my own demand, that is, I demanded a wife who could obey my arrangement. Then I practiced my thinking to meet the needs of others. I knew that my wife really turned to me for help because of deficiency, so I should meet her need. Finally, I entrusted two fears: 1. I accepted the situation that the child might get cold, and thought it would be fine to just put on more clothes on the child. 2. I told myself that if my wife kept asking me for help capriciously like that in the future, I would also accept it, since none of the future situations were real, so I would always choose to satisfy her request for help and take action.

When I finished practicing the above thought patterns, I agreed on the wife's request. And then, my wife was happy and awoke the kid, and waited for her to fully wake up, and we set off together.

Just as I was driving along, I repeated all the thoughts I had just practiced if I felt the mood of resistance, so that I kept my mind in the peaceful miracle mind all the way. (I was repeatedly resistant because I had just learned the theories about answering people's request for help and getting peaceful situations, and it was the first time I had put these theories into practice, so my practice was a little unstable.)

The affair went on. When we got to the doctor's house, the doctor diagnosed my mother-in-law's illness, and then prescribed a prescription. The affair was over, and we could leave after we got the prescription. But this was just the beginning of things. After the doctor finished the diagnose for my mother-in-law, he began to tease my child, but during the process of teasing the child, the doctor found the problem, looking at my child's fingers (traditional Chinese doctor pediatrics diagnosis sometimes depends on the situation of children's fingers), he said to us, "your child ate too much and suffers from indigestion, and currently has a fever". Only then did we find out that the child was really feverish, and her face was very hot and red. The doctor asked us what we fed the child in the past few days. Did she eat much? We answered that all the food was noodles, and the child had eaten a lot every day prior to a few days ago. When the doctor heard this, he told us, "now, a child who is one and a half years old does not know what is full and what is hungry. Even if the child is full, you continue to feed her and she will still eat. So your child has indigestion and is having a fever". (My family and I had no idea that the child couldn't distinguish from hunger and fullness, and us adults loved the child, so when that kid ate more than she could, we were happy.

Then, the doctor told me to go to a nearby pharmacy store to buy a medicine for child's indigestion. I went there at once, and I got the baby's medicine as soon as I got to the pharmacy. But when I bought the medicine, I found that this pharmacy store also sold Chinese herbal medicine, and I thought that my wife still needed two kinds of Chinese herbal medicine, so incidentally I asked the pharmacist whether they had those two kinds of Chinese herbal medicine. The pharmacist said yes, and I bought it as soon as I heard it. Then I went back to the doctor's house with the medicines.

After I came back to the doctor's house, the doctor immediately fed my child the medicine, but this medicine was bitter for my child, she choked on the bitter taste and coughed when she had taken half of the medicine. She started to vomit and vomited out all the food in her stomach. The doctor was glad to see the child vomit and said to us, "the child will be much better if she vomits the food out". Then the child started to cry because of vomiting. With the crying, the child started to vomit again. This time, the child vomited out a kind of transparent mucus. The doctor was even more pleased when he saw it, and said to us, "When the child has vomited out this transparent mucus, the child has recovered and the fever will be gone in a few minutes. Because the child's indigestion will cause stomach fire, fire will produce sputum, and sputum will accumulate in the lungs and form inflammation, which is the cause of your child's fever, but your child has already vomited out food and sputum, so she will not have internal heat and inflammation, and she does not need to take medicine". Sure enough, after another hour, my child's fever was gone. At last, the doctor told us not to feed the baby too much at dinner, so we thanked the doctor and drove home.

However, as I was driving home, I suddenly realized that the consequence of taking my child to the doctor's house was too much of a surprise. Because before we left, none of us knew that the child had indigestion. It was then that I realized the peaceful situation and ending brought by the miracle mind was everybody's happiness. Firstly, my child's illness was diagnosed inexplicably and cured quickly. Secondly, I learned not to feed the kid too much, which saved me a lot of trouble in the future. Thirdly, my mother-in-law went to see doctor on her own so that she would not be misdiagnosed. Fourthly, my wife's two flavors of medicine which she lacked were obtained. Fifthly, my family and child escaped the adversity of going to the hospital at night. (This one is quite impressive for me. If my child had a high fever at night, my family and I would take her to the emergency department of Tianjin children's hospital, but the children's hospital in our city was full at night. That is to say, even if we got to the hospital, we also needed to queue up for several hours to see the doctor, and taking the child to see the doctor entails at least 2 to 3 adults to accompany the child, because queuing is needed for registration, testing, infusion for reducing the fever. So for people in our city, it is a real pain to bring the kids to emergency treatment at night. And most critically, doctors in the hospital may not be able to diagnose a fever caused by indigestion. The following troubles are evident.) When I thought about this, I realized the benefits I had gained and what adversity I had avoided. On the way home, I marveled at the incredibility of these modes of thinking and the peaceful miracle mind; at the same time, I have completely trusted them.

This case illustrates a passage in this part: the miracle mind will manifest a new situation of peace to for you to experience, and this new peaceful situation will directly replace a situation that the sub-consciousness has already designed for you. To specify, when you practice this new thought system and get a miracle mind during the process of experiencing a certain life scene, this state of mind will immediately or gradually manifest a new peaceful situation for you to experience, and at the same time, the adversity that your sub-consciousness has already designed for you will disappear immediately or gradually. Then your destiny has been changed. And when you have experienced this peaceful situation, you will not only be deeply aware that you have avoided some adversity, but also be surprised that this peaceful situation brings you such a happy and unexpected ending, which alone can be called a miracle.

There is a Chinese saying that 'misfortune may be an actual blessing'. This proverb answers the question you may be asking, and the meaning of this proverb more or less represents the meaning of a miracle mind and a peaceful situation. So, it is up to you to choose whether you want to practice this thinking pattern that will enable you to achieve the miracle mind and the peaceful situation.

Finally, in order to make you more clearly cognizant of the benefits of the mode of thinking presented in this part, I will give an extended illustration on the example of the quarrel between the young couple.

1. If you are the wife in this case, how can you be sure that it is not beneficial that your husband plays games. Maybe after a week, your husband will say to you, "fortunately, I played games at home every day, so I didn't go out to drink with my friends. If I had gone, I would have suffered traffic accident with them yesterday". When you hear these words, do you still think your husband is wrong to play games every day?

2. If you are the husband in this case, how can you be sure it is not beneficial that your wife won't let you play games? Maybe you would meet a bunch of stupid teammates while playing games, and then you would get mad at them There are such examples in the world. Would you say it is wrong for your wife to stop you from playing games?

3. If you are the husband in the case, how can you be certain that it is wrong for your wife to ask you to go shopping with her? If you did not go shopping but to drink with friends, you might have suffered the traffic accident with your friends.

Therefore, there is a saying in the world, "if I knew it, I would listen to you". Or, to put it another way: "there is no use regretting". How profound these two sentences are.

As a narrator I am not threatening you with all of these, but I am just trying to tell you that people have no evaluative ability (except in the fields of work and law), because things that you now consider right may turn out to be wrong over time, while things that you now consider wrong may turn out to be right over time. There are also things that you have judged differently for several times over time. So, the evaluation of people's mind is very unstable, and this evaluation is only an illusion of the mind when you take the world as real, which doesn't harness your life, nor change your life, because it would only continually fluctuate with the vicissitudes of your life conditions and constantly change. Thus, people's evaluative ability makes it impossible for you to achieve the true peace and happiness.

So far, please have a thorough review of your own course of life, and you can think over whether your experiences through self-assertion and subjective evaluation have brought you true peace and happiness. If the answer is no, you can now choose to practice the new thought system by yourself, because this is the only thought system that will enable you to achieve true peace and happiness. The real case I am telling you aims to show you that once you have practiced that thought system and let go of self-assertion and subjective evaluation, your life won't get out of control. In addition, you will get the best peaceful ending.

At the end of this part, I will narrate a few matters needing attention to practice satisfying needs, since many situations in the world do not require you to apply the practice of satisfying needs that are discussed in this part.

1. As for people you don't know, if they put forward request beyond the scope of law, such as fraud or robbing of property, and so on, you can directly use the law of the country where you are to deal with it, especially when you face personal attack, you shall protect your body from harm as far as possible; if you can subdue him, just do it; if you can't, just try to run away, and turn to legal means as a last resort. Because the body is your main means for learning your last lesson in life. Don't give it up easily.

2. Sometimes people you do not know ask you for help within the scope of the law. As the saying goes, they need your help for a just cause or for their welfare. But there is a rare situation in this category, that is, they might frame you after getting your help, which can be simplified as 'blackmailing'. So when that happens, you can first think about it: whether the case laws or the guiding cases or the rules of custom of your country

can protect your well-meant actions and punish those possible blackmails. After you think about it, you can make your own choices. Because the world is so complex, and laws and enforcement vary from country to country, then sometimes your good intentions are not enough.

3. People you know ask you to do things that don't accord with the rules of the law. You needn't do it. For example, if someone you know has been hurt by someone, and he asks you to retaliate against that person, you can persuade him to use legal action first.

4. As for friends and relatives other than your immediate family members, if they ask you for help, they need you to do something, or they want to borrow money from you, you can consult with your immediate family members, especially your spouse, and then take action. Because the world is a collective body of family units, interpersonal relationships of immediate family members are more important than other ones.

5. If people you know ask you to hate and attack others, you can say no. Because the requirement is that you convict someone else. If this happens in your life, you can either brush it off or laugh it off. For example, when my wife badmouths another person in front of me, she wants me to think in the same way, and wants me to convict that person, too. At this time, I could say something like this in addition to slighting it over: "if I hate a person, I can find a reason to hate all people. So, I don't hate anybody including you". That has basically terminated the end of my wife's request. Over time, my wife has given it up.

6. The work category of the world, each has his own duty. Mutual help in the working category is the norm. It doesn't matter whether you apply the practice of satisfying needs.

7. If you are an adult and unemployed person, and your immediate family members want you to have a worldly job, then you may meet their needs, because this call for help is the manifestation of the previous deficiency in your sub-consciousness. But if you have already got a job and if your immediate family members want you to change the job, you may ignore their demands. Because it's your freedom to choose what you do

and it's your business, since you have the right to make the final decision in this matter. Simply speaking, the notice of this point is: If you don't have a job and your family wants you to look for one, you shall go look for one, but whatever you do is up to you.

8. When two people in your interpersonal relationship disagree and you are the final performer, or you are in the disagreement, you can wait for their unified opinion before acting. For specific correspondence for this situation, you can refer to the required reading "Function of the Holy Spirit and Concealment".

9. If someone who doesn't understand the laws of nature needs your help and does something against the laws of nature, you can ignore his demands. For example, if a naive child asks you to put his hand in the hot pot, you should not listen to him. This category is basically targeted at children who have not learned the objective laws of human life.

The core content of this new thought system is the combined application of true forgiveness, giving innocence, letting go of needs, entrusting and satisfying needs narrated in this part. There is only one requirement for the combined use of these thoughts, that is, to lead by example, because only if you do it first can your inner peace be perceived by others. Only then were they likely to pro-actively ask and learn your thinking patterns. So, in life, you don't even have to scold others when practicing this thought system, "If you take the world as real, you will not perform true forgiveness and you will be unlucky". Because such accusations mean you have taken the person in front of you as real and convicted him with mean intimidation. This is the end of this part.

September 2017

6 Sacrifice and Asking for Nothing in Return

In this part, I will illustrate the connotations and application of 'sacrifice' and asking for nothing in return. This time, I will still use the case of the quarrel between the young couple to make an extensive demonstration. The case is as follows.

There is a family of two. The husband and wife are both salary workers. One day, the husband got infatuated with online games. He just played games after coming back home every day. This made his wife upset. Then, a few days later, the wife could not stand it any longer, and she scolded his husband when he was playing games, "you only know play games every day, and ignore me. You go to live with the person in the game if you continue playing! Turn it off now!" When the husband heard this, he immediately got angry and answered, "What's wrong with me playing games after work? Leave me alone and don't make trouble". Then, the wife got angrier, went on to say: "How long has it been since the last time you accompanied me to go shopping? Accompany me shopping now. If you keep on playing, I will smash the computer". Then the husband continued to fight back, "smash it, I won't go". At that time, the wife saw that the attack was useless, she said to the husband, "I wash clothes and cook for you every day. I treat you like my lord every day. Can't I ask you to come shopping with me?" But the husband continued to fight back to say, "I make money every day and I am so tired; can't see how hard I work for this family? And you are still not satisfied." This is the end of story.

I will analyze the connotations of the last two sentences in the case. Take the wife as an example. She thought about it before saying that sentence, "You did a lot of things that I hated during my time with you, and all that was because of your selfishness and wrong ideas. But I did not attack and punish you for your mistakes, because I was kind. I stayed with you even thought you did so many wrongs, I tolerated your mistakes and silently did good things for you. I chose to do so in the hope that you would repent and repay me. But you ignored my patience and devotion, and you didn't even want to do small things for me, such as go shopping with me. You are so abominable". These are the thoughts that initiated the wife's last remarks "I wash clothes and cook for you every day......".

In life, many words and thoughts are similar to those of the last two sentences of the dialogue in the case. For example, "I have been living with you for a long time and I have been so good to you, but how did you treat me?" Or, "I have done so much for you, I only wish you could change a little, but why don't you change? My efforts have been wasted". Or, "I have been perfectly fulfilled both in love and duty. Since I cannot reform you, then you should go die! I will never do things for you again". I suppose you would not be unfamiliar with those words and thoughts, and these words and thoughts are the sacrifice that is talked about in this part.

What is sacrifice? Sacrifice is that you have already regarded some thoughts and acts of the other party as guilty and punishable and those thoughts and acts have made you a victim. But at that time, you don't attack the other directly, because you choose another form. You put up with sins first and try to reform the other in doing things for them. It is as if you were telling the other party that your efforts and your sufferings are caused by their sin, and all that you have done is for atoning for them. Your giving then becomes a means of attack, and the other party feels a sense of guilt that you give them. Then, you use that guilt to raise demands on the other party. The attributes of these demands are the returns you ask for your efforts. That is sacrifice.

So what is the ending of sacrifice? There are two kinds of endings:

1. If the other party has identified his sins and confessed themselves, the other party will satisfy your various demands. At that time, the other party is virtually atoning for their own sin, and your mind will gain temporary balance.

2. If the other party ignores the guilt and contributions you have given them and will not confess themselves or give returns for your contributions. Then you will have a great fear that your efforts will never be rewarded.

The fear is then increasingly amplified by your incessant efforts. In the end, when the fear reaches its ultimate limit, you will stop giving and turn directly to anger and attack, or you attack while giving. If the other party is still unrepentant, you will punish or abandon the other party. Certainly, if the guilt you give to the other party is too strong, and the demands you raise are too overwhelming for the other party to bear, they will be exceptionally frightened, and then they will abandon you. This is the second ending of sacrifice.

Let me give you one more example from life to better illustrate sacrifice. There must be a kind of emotional mediation program on TV in your country, and that kind of program must have the scenes like this:

1. There was a mother and a son on the show. The mother said, "My child didn't behave himself when he was young. He indulged in eating, drinking and gambling, and did nothing good. There was no use teaching him, and finally he got himself imprisoned. However, during his years in prison, as his mother, I never gave him up. All these years, I have been working hard to make money, because I wanted to give him a better future. And every time I visited my child, I told him how hard I worked and what I expected of him. In the end, it paid off. After my child was released from prison, he understood my hardship and effort, and his guilt, too. Then, he thoroughly rectified his previous errors. Now he has a formal job and is very filial to me. He has become a good son now, and my efforts have not been in vain.

When the host and the audience heard it, they said, "look! This is the maternal love of the world, how great! This kid is the model of prodigal son turning back. What a loving family!

2. There was a mother and a son on the show. The mother said, "My child didn't behave himself when he was young. He indulged in eating, drinking and gambling, and did nothing good. There was no use teaching him, and finally got himself imprisoned. However, during his years in prison, as his mother, I never gave him up. All these years, I have been working hard to make money, because I want to give him a better future.

And every time I visited my child, I told him how hard I worked and what I expected of him. But after he got out of jail, he still indulged in the bad habits as before. I introduced a job to him, which he just did it for a while but then gave it up. I am so sad that all my efforts have been wasted".

The host and the audience showed great hatred after hearing it. Then the host began to insanely scold this youngster, for being unfilial, senseless, and indecent. Even the TV audiences gnashed the teeth in anger, on the brink of jumping onto the stage and slapping the youngster.

These two opposite scenes illustrate the connotations of sacrifice and two endings. Perhaps you will say isn't that the mother and son have "love" good? Yes, on the surface it seems good, but this superficial goodness does not dissolve the guilt that the mother has given to her son; that is to say, the guilt must be manifested as a circumstance of being sacrificed for the mother to experience. And this superficial goodness does not dissolve the guilt that the son has given to himself, which means that the son will sooner or later be bitter due to incessant recompense (atonement). Therefore, the superficial goodness of the relationship between the mother and the son is only a temporary goodness, because they cannot escape the rules of the working of sins and guilt. There are too many such examples and words in the world, for example, one party may say, "Dare you not listen to me, have you forgotten those mistakes you made in the past? Don't forget how I used to treat you?" The other party replied, "I have been kind to you all these years. Why do you keep grabbing at my past?" This is the ending that the sense of sacrifice brings to both parties. The connotation of this ending is that the guilty party thinks he has redeemed his sins, but the sacrificial party does not think so, and at that time the two parties will incessantly compare and seesaw their efforts. However, these comparisons and seesaws cannot dissolve the guilt, instead they will consolidate the authenticity of sins in both people's minds. This is a trick of how the sense of sacrifice makes sins real.

To sum up, sacrifice is just another kind of pattern of conviction, and the two parties manipulated by the sense of sacrifice will sooner or later convert sacrifice into mutual attack. For example, when the husband in the case felt the sacrifice of his wife, he immediately experienced the guilt that the wife gave to him, and then pushed the guilt directly back and expressed his own sacrifice. So he said, "I am so tired of making money every day. Can't you see the hard work I have done for this family? And you are still not satisfied".

Most of the reasons for divorce in the world come from this sense of sacrifice. In life, both men and women think they have put up with each other's mistakes. Both men and women think they have done a lot for each other. But finally both men and women think they have not gained the corresponding return. In this way, the sacrifices of both parties gradually turn to anger and mutual attack, eventually mutual abandonment.

In addition to divorce, the sense of sacrifice pervades in all areas of relationships. For example, people often teach children and say, "I have signed you up for so many classes, including dance class, piano class, but why are you not eager to learn?" When the child hears these words, it doesn't matter what he answers. What matters is that the child's expressions after hearing these words are definitely unhappy. Why is that? Because these words mean that you have given the guilt to the child. But who is willing to accept that guilt in the world?

I am not going to list other cases, because the cases of sacrifices are quite common in life. If you observe life very carefully, you will find that the sense of sacrifice is ingrained in everybody's mind. So, how to break away from the sense of sacrifice becomes a lesson you must learn. In the following, I will put you into the roles of wife and husband.

First of all, I will put you into the role of wife. If you are the wife in this case, the first step is to wake yourself up in a quarrel. Then you need to practice all of the thinking patterns described in the previous parts: true forgiveness, giving innocence, letting go of needs (including the needs of shopping), and entrustment of fear. At that time, your husband and you will become a peaceful miracle mind. And then this time, you have to be alert to the sense of sacrifice within you, and you have to think when you are vigilant:

1. The things my husband used to do to hurt me were only some circumstances in my dream, and he used to be only an image in my dream, so he was guiltless in the past and is guiltless now.

2. All my past contributions to him were to satisfy his sincere request for help, so I will not ask for changes and rewards from my husband. I won't cling to the past contributions any more.

When you have completed the above thoughts and done nothing, your sense of sacrifice will melt away, along with the sense of guilt you gave to your husband. Then your husband won't experience the sense of guilt. Up to now, your mind will be firmly united in a state of miracle mind. This state of mind will then present you with a peaceful circumstance, similar to the one described in the previous one, except that you will not experience a new circumstance of being sacrificed, because this time you do not use sacrificial thinking to convict your husband. This is thinking and application of overcoming sacrifices while asking for nothing in return.

The principle of overcoming sacrifices and asking for nothing in return is as follows: you first have to forgive the other party for the things they have done that hurt you in the past, so that you can dissolve sins you have convicted towards the other party in the past. Then, on that basis, you can turn your past contributions into satisfying the other party's genuine pleas for help. The guilt you gave to the other will be taken back and dissolved by you. This is the thought to be practiced by the sacrificial party. This practice also has another assistant thinking, that is, you can recall more good things that the other party did to you in the past, for which they did not expect repay from you. This will make it easier for you to practice thinking patterns that overcome sacrifice and ask for nothing in return. (In more intimate relationships, both sides must have done a lot of things to help each other expecting nothing in return, because you would not have formed intimate relationships without these things, then the thought of remembering only the good in people and forgiving the bad is of great assistance to the practice of overcoming sacrifices and asking for nothing in return.)

The next step is to put you into the role of the husband, but first of all, I will remind you that the husband's situation in the case is different from the wife's situation, because the husband is the recipient of the sacrifice and the requested party, so he uses a different thinking pattern because of his different situation.

If you are the husband in this case, the first step you should take is to be aware, and you should be aware of your sense of sacrifice. Then you can practice all the thinking modes illustrated in the former parts: true forgiveness, giving innocence, letting go of needs and entrustment of fear, but you don't use the thinking to meet others' sincere request for help first, because this time the request for help your wife put forward is also mixed with the sacrifice of your wife and the guilt she gives to you. So, you should think like this:

1. The things my wife used to do to hurt me were only some circumstances in my dream, and she used to be only an image in my dream, so she used to be and is innocent.

2. All my contributions I did to her in the past were to satisfy her sincere request for help, so I will not ask for changes and returns from my wife, and I will not cling to those contributions in the past.

3. The guilt my wife gave me because of her sacrifice is non-existent, because she and I are innocent. So, I can't have any guilt.

4. If the guilt my wife gave me because of her sacrifice is non-existent, then the request my wife makes for me is only a sincere request for help, so I will satisfy her request for help.

The above thoughts are the ones to be practiced by the recipient of sacrifices. From these thoughts, you can see that you, as the recipient of sacrifices, needs to practice two more steps than the sacrificial party, namely the third and fourth steps. This is because you can turn the demands mixed with senses of sacrifices into genuine pleas for help only when you first forgive the guilt that the sacrificial party gave to you. Otherwise, you are likely to push the guilt back to the sacrificial party and express your sacrifices. Besides, if you don't, you will experience the fear that the sacrificial party will cling to your sins forever and worry that they will make countless demands on you. So, when you are faced with sacrifices, the first thing you have to do is to use true forgiveness to dissolve the guilt that the sacrificial party gave to you. This is the crucial step of practice for the recipient of the sacrifices, and the core of this part.

But if you are still fearful that your wife will continue to express sacrifices to you in the future after you have done all of the above thinking, then you can practice the thinking of entrustment of fear again. You can think like this: In the future, if my wife frequently expresses sacrifices to me and make demands on me, I will ceaselessly forgive her for the guilt she gave me, and ceaselessly satisfy her heartfelt pleas for help". After such entrustment, all your fear will disappear, and then your mind will be unified in miracle mind, but this time because you are the recipient of sacrifices and the requested party, after you have practiced these above thoughts and acts, your peace will be extended to your wife's heart, and then the peace will bring your wife this cognizance: "my efforts are not in vain. I get rewards from my husband, and I can feel that the reward is just my husband's love to me. I am very happy". Your wife's sense of deprivation, fear and sacrifice will disappear. Up to now, one of your troubles has been rid of. In the end, you will acquire a peaceful situation due to the miracle mind. This situation is similar to that described in the previous part, but there is one more thing, if you, as the husband, are able to apply the four thoughts described above for a long time to handle the sacrifices of your wife, then your wife's sense of sacrifice for you will become less and less, and eventually the sense of sacrifice will be completely gone. Then your wife won't raise demands on you due to her sacrifices for you. This is long-term peaceful situation that the recipient of sacrifices will eventually get if they have applied the proper thoughts.

Moreover, as the recipient of sacrifices, if you can regularly use the right thinking to meet the demands of the sacrificial party, you will not hate and abandon the sacrificial party. Then in the future, those who are not abandoned by you (the sacrificial side) will certainly bring you some great benefits. Simply speaking, these people who are not abandoned by you will help you out when you are in troubles. This is another kind of peaceful situation that can be obtained by the recipient of sacrifices. When this happens, you will understand all the values of overcoming sacrifices and asking for nothing in return.

At the end of this part, I will clarify why you should ask for nothing in return, because when you have practiced this mode of thinking and do not ask for anything in return, you will become a miracle mind without any sense of deficiency, and all the peaceful circumstances you will obtain are also manifested by this miracle mind. So, the peaceful miracle mind is the most perfect reward you will gain, and that is the true meaning of asking for nothing in return.

Finally, as an explicator, I would like to say to you, "do not think that what I am saying will make you a weak person in life; you should not think so. True strength does not lie in the external, but in the heart. You may give everyone the superficial impression that you are an outwardly powerful person all along, but does outward power really work? Are you really happy? Do you really have no troubles? So, it is up to you to decide whether you shall practice this thinking pattern that will make your mind incredibly powerful.

October 2017

7 Punishment and Forgiveness

In this part, I will talk about punishment and forgiveness. I still use the case of the quarrel between the young couple and extend the example to illustrate the theme. The case is as follows:

There is a family of two. The husband and wife are both salary workers. One day, the husband became infatuated with online games. He played games after coming back home every day. This made his wife upset. Then, a few days later, the wife could not stand it any longer, and then scolded her husband when he played games, "you play games every day, and ignore me. You go to live with the person in the game if you continue playing! Turn it off now!" When the husband heard this, he immediately got angry and answered, "What's wrong with me playing games after work? Leave me alone and don't make troubles". Then, the wife got madder, and continued to say: "how long has it been since the last time you accompanied me to go shopping? Accompany me to go shopping now. If you go on playing, I will smash the computer". Then the husband continued to fight back, "smash it, I won't go". At that time, the wife saw that her attack was useless, and said to the husband, "I wash clothes and cook for you everyday. I treat you like the lord every day. Can't I ask you to accompany me to go shopping?" But after hearing that, the husband continued to fight back, "I make money everyday and I am so tired, you can't see how hard I work for this family? And you are still not satisfied". Finally the wife thoroughly got angry, saying, "ok, just play! I will post everything that you and I quarrel about in "Wechat Moments " (something like twitter) in a moment and show your ugly mug to your dad, mom, friends and family". When the husband heard this, he was also angry, saying, "How dare you! If you dare to post it in "Wechat Moments", I will not accompany you to go shopping. If I would accompany you to go shopping in the future, I would rather be hit to death by car". This is the end of story.

What to be illustrated is the last two threatening sentences in the case. First of all, I will define the nature of punishment: punishment is an attack against a crime, so punishment is conviction. Secondly, I will define the form of punishment: when you are going to punish a person, you first think about what he possesses and values (these things also include all the relationships that he has). Then, you will pick out the things that you can control and destroy (those that the other party owns and values). Finally, you will think about how you can destroy them, or how you can cut them out of the other party's life. If the other party loses these things, he will have a huge sense of deficiency and pain, and then you realize the goal of punishment, which is the fixed form of punishment. In the end, I will define the role of punishment: punishment is a means to force the other party to make concessions to you or change for you, and it can also be used as a form of intimidation.

The wife in the case just figured out one of her husband's cherished things according to the above thinking, namely: the self-image of her husband in front of friends and relatives, Then the wife came up with a way to ruin her husband's self-image by posting the quarrel affair in "Wechat Moments" and letting all relatives and friends see what they quarreled about. If all the relatives and friends knew about their quarrel, her husband would go through a situation where his friends and relatives ridiculed him. This situation would damage the husband's self-image and bring him pain and embarrassment. That is the kind of punishment she was going to use. And it was used as a tool of intimidation by his wife.

So what is the ending of punishment and intimidation? As for this case, there are usually two endings:

1. Her husband would give in to her due to his fear for her, but simultaneously, her husband would hide his hatred in his heart. At that time, the wife would begin to worry that her husband would take away and destroy what she had and valued.

2. For the scene in the case, when the husband heard his wife's words of punishment, he immediately realized that he was going to be a laughing

stock. He experienced sense of deficiency, fear, and victimhood at that time. And those emotions turned into anger and hatred in an instant. Then, the husband took the steps of revenge and counter-threat, saying, "How dare you? If you dare to post it in "Wechat Moments" (similar to twitter), and if I would accompany you to go shopping again, I would be hit to death by car". The connotation of the revenge is that the husband knew what the wife cherished was a husband that could accompany her.

In the world, there are similar scenes. Two more examples will be shown.

1. The child did not do homework, and the adult said to the child, "today, if you do not do the homework, you cannot eat". The child replied, "ok, I don't have to eat. I won't do homework".

The adult wanted to punish the child with hunger and wished them to be obedient. But the child used the behavior of not doing homework to revenge the adult, because the child understood that what the adult valued was an obedient good child.

2. A couple quarreled, and the husband failed in the quarrel, then he slammed the door, walked away from home with anger and had not gone back for several days, waiting for the wife to give up. But the wife did not give up, or look for the husband, instead went out for a shopping spree.

The husband punished his wife by running away from home, because he knew that his wife cherished a husband who came home every day. But the wife did not compromise, but revenged the husband by spending money, because she knew what the husband valued was the deposit money.

The above two cases represent the punishment and revenge that are on show every day in the world, and these two cases show that punishment and revenge only appear in the field of interpersonal relations. So how to overcome punishment and confront revenge (handling the situation of being punished) is a lesson you must learn. I will put you into the role of wife and husband and illustrate respectively.

First of all, I will put you into the party who initiated the punishment. For instance, you are the wife in the case, your first measures should be to wake yourself up during the quarrel and practice true forgiveness, giving innocence, letting go of needs, entrustment of fear, overcoming sacrifices and asking for nothing in return elaborated on in the previous parts. But this time, you need to be alert to the sense of punishment within yourself while practicing. After alerting yourself, you should think like this: "punishment is conviction. If I punish my husband, the guilt will be kept in my sub-consciousness and it will manifest a punishable situation for me to experience, so I will not punish my husband". When you think like this, the concept of punishment within you will disappear, and you will not experience a new situation of being punished in the future. Then one of your troubles has been rid of.

But if you post the affair in the "Wechat Moments" without alertness during the quarrel, and then you wake yourself up, what should you do? When this happens, you can withdraw the form of punishment after alerting yourself and practicing these above thoughts, i.e., you may delete the information in "Wechat Moments". This action represents that you have stopped the punishment.

These are the thought patterns that the party that initiated the punishment needs to practice. In the following, I will put you into the role of being punished and intimidated, but first I should make it clear that the emergence of this role often follows two premises:

1. This role often fails to respond to a genuine request for help and has attacked the other person before he or she is punished. Then, the other person resents him and initiates punishment.

2. The punished role used to punish others in the past; that is to say, he used punishment (sometimes across transmigration) to convict others, and then sins fermented the guilt and manifested situation of being punished for him to experience.

As you can see from both of these premises, the situation of being punished is just a manifestation of some previous guilt within the sub-consciousness. So, if you are the husband in the case, punishment and intimidation are likely to befall you because of previous sins even if you have practiced all the thoughts elaborated on in the previous parts. For example, although you practiced true forgiveness and other skillful thoughts during the quarrel and also accompanied your wife to go shopping, the guilt within your sub-conscious still manifested the following situation: your wife still hated you while shopping in the mall, and she still kept intimidating you and angrily posted it in "Wechat Moments". Then what are you going to do? When that happens, you certainly mustn't quarrel with her again and stop her punishing behavior. Because if you attack her again, it only represents that you have taken an image within your dream seriously and degenerated into the conviction mode. So as the punished one, you just have to learn how to deal with intimidation and punishment.

The thought of dealing with intimidation and punishment is the same as the entrustment of fear. You should think like this: "1. If my wife have posted it in "Wechat Moments", just let her do it, because I would face and accept any future situation. I am not a body, and I do not need the self-image in the world. 2. It doesn't matter if I would experience a situation of being ridiculed, because it is just a fantasized situation manifested by previous sins within my sub-consciousness, so I am not a victim even if I have experienced that situation". This is the application of the thoughts in the face of intimidation and punishment, which requires that you let go of everything you cherish and accept all adversities both mentally and physically, including the loss of self-dignity and various personality adversities. Then, you will not be afraid of the other party's intimidation and will calmly face the situation of being punished.

According to this situation, if your wife finally posted it in "Wechat Moments", you can practice true forgiveness ceaselessly in a situation of being punished as the method of handling every ridicule. This kind of ceaseless forgiveness will slowly dissolve previous sins in your sub-consciousness. And those ceaseless practices will continue to express the connotation for your wife that you are not a body, and cannot be a victim. At that time, the peace you own will ceaselessly extend to your wife's heart, and then the peace will bring your wife this cognizance: "my husband is really outstanding, and my punishment is useless to him; he doesn't have the slightest feeling of being a victim; his mind is so peaceful that there is no use punishing him". At this time, your wife's hatred of you increasingly diminishes. This is the thought and action to be practiced by the punished party.

To sum up, when you face and experience situations of being punished, you may ceaselessly apply the thought of true forgiveness to face the adversities of being punished. This practice can dissolve previous sins in your sub-consciousness. To take another example: your wife always holds the grudge about something you did in the past. She will lash out at you whenever she thinks about it and will launch a kind of physical punishment against you, that is, asking you to clean the floor every time when she feels angry. What should you do when that happens? Certainly, you have to clean the floor again and again, but in the process of cleaning, you should think like this: "my experience of this situation is only an illusory adversity manifested by a previous sin in my sub-consciousness, and my physical strength and fatigue does not really exist, so I will be willing to experience the situation". When you act in this way with forgiveness, your wife's hatred will increasingly diminish, so that the hatred will completely disappear one day, and some previous sin in your sub-consciousness and your wife's punishment for you will disappear along with the hatred. This is the internal connection between the situation of being punished and true forgiveness.

Finally, a few more clarifications about the practice of confronting punishment:

1. If someone you don't know initiates punishment to you, you may use the law to deal with it.

2. Punishment in the field of work is conducted according to the work rules, so in most cases, punishment in the work has nothing to do with the guilt within the sub-consciousness.

3. The persons who are able to punish you are usually core members of your family, but if your family members want you to hurt your body,

you can refuse. For example, if one of your family members wants you to mutilate yourself or kill yourself, you can refuse because your body is a tool for you to learn the truth and you don't have to give up easily.

4. You can proceed to legal settlement if your family members commit domestic violence against you.

In the end, I will also ask a question on behalf of you, which will be put forward by the husband in the case, namely: "if my wife posted it in "Wechat Moments", although I could forgive everyone's ridicule and accusations, what should I do when people around me blame my wife? For example, if my parents knew about our quarrel, they would blame and hate my wife. Then how can I deal with the bad relationship between them?" The answer to this question will be elaborated on in the next part. Because the way you respond to this situation is also a lesson that you must learn: how do you deal with the love and hate relationship of those around you? This is the end of the part.

November 2017

8 The Role of Holy Spirit and Concealment

Continued from the preceding part, first there will be illustration of how you face love and hatred relationships between people around you, and then I will talk about the disadvantages of concealment and how to overcome concealment.

In this part, I still use the example of couple quarrel and add a character to the case. The case is as follows:

There is a family of three, a husband, a wife and a 20-year-old child. The husband and the wife are both salary workers. One day, the husband became infatuated with online games. He just played games after coming back home every day. This made his wife upset. Then, a few days later, the wife could not stand it any longer, and then scolded her husband when he played games, "you play games only every day, and ignore me. You go to live with the person within the game if you continue playing! Turn it off now!" When the husband heard this, he immediately got angry and answered, "What's wrong with me playing games after work? Leave me alone and don't make trouble". Then, the wife got angrier, continuing to say: "How long has it been since the last time you accompanied me to go shopping? Accompany me shopping now. If you keep on playing, I will smash the computer". Then the husband continued to fight back, "smash it, I won't go". At that time, the wife saw that attack was useless, and said to the husband, "I wash clothes and cook for you every day. I treat you like the lord every day. Can't I ask you to accompany me to go shopping?" But the husband continued to fight back and said, "I make money every day and am so tired, you can't see how hard I work for this family? And you are still not satisfied". Finally the wife thoroughly got angry, saying, "ok, just play! I will post everything that you and I argue about in "Wechat Moments" (such as twitter) and show your ugly mug to your dad, mom, relatives and friends". When the husband heard this, he got very angry, saying, "How dare you! If you dare to post it in "Wechat Moments", I would rather be hit by a car than go shopping with you. So, they began a sustained quarrel, and their child saw them quarrel. This is the end of the story.

I am going to put you directly into the role of the child in this illustration, because the child in this case is facing the love and hatred relationship between his parents.

If you are the child in this case, how do you handle the quarrel between your parents? First, you should practice the idea of true forgiveness and giving innocence. You should think about it in this way: "my parents are just two illusory images that I dream of. The real ones of them are the sons of god, guiltless and innocent, so the event of their attack against each other doesn't exist for me or for them". When you think like that, your parents and you will be a peaceful miracle mind.

Then, you will continue to practice entrustment of fear, because you will develop some fear because of their quarrel. For example, you may be afraid of living in a hostile environment, or you may be afraid that their constant quarrel will break up the family. So, the practice of entrustment of fear is an imperative part of the practices the role should perform.

Entrustment of fear will teach you to think like this: "if my parents quarrel every day, even if they finally get divorced, I will accept it. I accept it. Because none of these circumstances are true; I am not a victim even though I have experienced them". When you have entrusted the fear like that, you will be in a state of fearless miracle mind and be inspired to do the right thing by that miracle mind. The inspiration is: "you just see their quarrel silently. You don't have to do anything".

However, this event will not end immediately due to your practice, because your parents will not stop quarreling because of your silent practices. But the key thing that will happen is that your practice will invite out the Holy Spirit within you, and the intangible Holy Spirit will automatically work in your parents' minds and give them some inspirations to do the right thing because you have actively practiced the above thoughts. Specifically, your parents will think in the quarrel and after quarrel that "why I quarrel with him/her? There is nothing wrong with him/her. He/

she is such a good person, and I don't have to change him/her". Then, their quarrel will not get worse, and their quarrel will evolve into a harmonious ending. This is the working pattern and function of the Holy Spirit. The principle of this pattern is as follows: when you face the conflict between people around you, if you first practice true forgiveness, give innocence and entrustment, then you can extend the pure innocence into the minds of both parties to the conflict, and the place where there is pure innocence is the holy spirit's habitat, so the Holy Spirit will automatically operate in the minds of both parties and will give them some correct inspirations to do things due to your practices. At this time, the thinking and actions of both parties in conflict will undergo some positive change (The explanation in this paragraph can be understood with reference to the fourth part.).

To highlight the function of the Holy Spirit, I will show a few more secular solutions to conflicts between other people's, which will bring you a clear contrast.

1. When you confront the conflict between the people around you, you dissuade both parties from fighting each other and affirm that there are mistakes on both parties, and then you ask both parties to correct their mistakes. This approach represents that you have already convicted both parties.

2. You might take one side and affirm that the other party is wrong. It is also a conviction.

3. You might recognize one party's sacrifices and demand the other party to change, which is also a conviction.

4. You might try to stop their quarrel by expressing sacrifices. For example, you might say, "I have been nice to both of you. Give me face. Stop fighting". It is also a conviction.

5. You might try to stop the conflict by attacking both parties. It is also a conviction.

To sum up, the secular approaches cannot resolve conflicts, instead it will lose you in the mode of conviction. Most importantly, you don't have any ability of evaluation when you face conflict with other people. Because:

1. Conflicts between other people are illusory to you, and the nature of illusion is meaningless and neither right nor wrong.

2. It is impossible for you to fully understand all the causes and historical backgrounds of the conflict, including previous transmigrations of both parties.

3. It is impossible to know how many differences there are between the two parties of a conflict in terms of worldview, outlook on life and values.

4. You can't evaluate the result of your active dissuasion and correction of these conflicts (except in the field of work).

So, giving up subjective evaluation is the first step in confronting the conflicts between other people. Then you can practice true forgiveness and giving innocence and entrustment of fear alone. That is enough. You should do what you can do, and that's all. At that time, the Holy Spirit will automatically work in the minds of "the targets of your practices" and give them some inspirations to do the right things. This is a fixed pattern of facing the conflict between others, which can be summed up as: as long as you do your best, the Holy Spirit will do his best to fulfill his duty of correction. Correcting other people's conflicts is the duty of the Holy Spirit, not yours. So you don't have to correct other people's minds. If one party of the conflict actively consults you about a solution to the conflict, you can actively offer some positive advices, but until then, you can be waiting patiently.

These illustrations are the answers to "how you should deal with the love and hatred relationship between those around you". But you don't suppose that they are easy to do in life. You might say, "in the future, when my parents quarrel, I will be able to maintain the thinking mode of true forgiveness, etc. Well, this situation might be easier for you. But what if your role isn't a child? For example:

1. If the child in the case is replaced by the mother of the husband, then you as the mother sees your son and daughter-in-law quarrel, will it be easy for you to practice the thinking illustrated in this part?

2. If the child in the case is replaced by the father of the wife, you, as the father see your daughter quarrel with your son-in-law, what do you do?

In the world, people are basically more concerned about the next generation, so it is easier to forgive the quarrels between the older generation in life, but not between peers or between the younger generation. Take another example. If your wife and your child quarrel, whose side do you take? Or if your wife and your child, and your parents engage in a dogfight, how do you confront it? So, don't think the above is easily done.

Next, I am going to try to answer two remaining questions in previous parts, so that you can understand more deeply about the function of the Holy Spirit.

1. When two people in your relationship disagree and you are the final executer, or you are involved in it, you can wait for them to agree before acting. (The remaining question of the fifth part)

I will use a simple example to illustrate it. For example, your family wants to travel abroad. Your wife wants to go to Germany, but your child wants to go to Japan. So, they have divergence. What should you do about it? When this happens, all you can do is to keep on applying the thoughts illustrated in this part. Because your practice will invite out the Holy Spirit, and then this intangible Holy Spirit will automatically work within their minds, and eventually you will see their divergence be resolved satisfactorily, or you will see other harmonious endings.

2. As for the remaining question in the last part, namely, the affair of "Wechat Moments" (like twitter), you may ask this question after you accept the punishment: "If my wife posts it in 'Wechat Moments' to punish me, I could forgive everyone's ridicule and accusations, but what should I do if people around me blame my wife? For example, if my parents knew

about our quarrel, they would accuse and hate my wife. Then, how should I deal with the bad relationship between them?"

The answer to this question is to apply the thinking illustrated in this part. If your parents start to hate your wife after seeing "Wechat Moments"(like twitter), or your parents have a direct conflict with your wife after seeing "Wechat Moments", you can practice the thinking model illustrated in this part before or during the conflict. You can start by forgiving these 3 people and giving them pure innocence, and then practice entrusting fear: "even if the three of them have been attacking each other for a long time, I accept it. I accept it. Because the situation that they hate each other and attack each other does not exist at all, and it is just a dream". After you practice like this, the Holy Spirit will automatically work in the hearts of them and give them some inspirations to do the right things, and then you will see their bad relationship become a harmonious one. This is the function of the Holy Spirit.

Finally, three more points about the function of the Holy Spirit shall be strengthened:

1. The Holy Spirit can only be invited out by a fearless mind, so when you face conflicts between others, you must practice the thought of entrustment in order to become the fearless miracle mind. This is the absolute premise of inviting out the Holy Spirit. There is no exception.

2. When there are drastic physical conflicts between people around you, or even worse, they pick up some utensils (such as bottles, family tools including kitchen knife, etc.) to fight with each other, then you can stop physical conflict between both parties in the first place provided your own security is guaranteed (if you cannot stop them, you shall ask the police to help prevent or stop their physical conflict by other means). Then, you can practice the thought illustrated in this part.

3. You can actively prevent self-mutilation and suicide by those around you due to conflict, because the body is an important tool to learn the truth for everyone.

In the following, I will begin to talk about the disadvantages of concealment and how to overcome concealment, because this is not only a lesson that you must learn, but also has a certain internal connection with the above explanations.

First of all, the nature of concealment will be defined: concealment is a mode of thinking that keeps the mind in a continual state of guilt and fear, so concealment is the most direct harm to the mind. Concealment is defined: when you do something, you consider that you can't tell someone about that, or can't tell anyone about that. Finally, several situations that will lead to concealment are presented:

1. You think you have done something that will be attacked and punished by someone, so you are afraid that someone knows about it.

2. You think you have done something to punish someone, but you don't want them to know about it because you are afraid of being retaliated.

3. In your relationships, a person around you asks you to do something for him, and that is sometimes what you have to do. However, when you do these things, you also consider that you have to conceal it from someone, because if what you do is to be known by someone, you will be attacked and punished.

These three situations basically indicate the connotations of concealment: you have done something wrong that cannot be told to others and plunge yourself into fear, mixed with convicting yourself or someone else. So, concealment is another form of conviction. These are the disadvantages of concealment.

Everyone in the world has done more or less things to be concealed, and these concealed things are the root cause of your current pain and annoyance. So, how to overcome concealment becomes a lesson that everyone must learn.

The actual method of overcoming concealment is generally not complicated, that is, before you do something, first you have to ask your heart, after you do it, whether you dare to tell it to all people, all people, no one being excluded. Then, you ask yourself: is there anyone around you who might fiercely object to this thing? If the answer is that you are brave enough to tell it to everyone (that doesn't mean you should actively tell it to everyone), and no one is against it, do it. If the answer is the opposite, don't do it. This is the major method to overcome concealment. However, this uncomplicated method is more complex when applied. Therefore, I will explain how to practice overcoming concealment in life according to the three situations just illustrated.

The first situation: "you affirm that you have done something that will be attacked and punished by someone". In this situation, you can simply apply the method of overcoming concealment, and then you have to consider why you have to do the concealed thing. The answer is so simple that it gives you something you desire. These desirable things sometimes come from physical entertainment, sometimes from mental satisfaction, and sometimes from the lure of money. So, in these situations, if you want to overcome concealment, you have to be willing to let go of these desires. I have illustrated how to let go of the desires, then you can apply the thought of true forgiveness and letting go of needs to dissolve the illusory sense of satisfaction and illusory sense of deprivation. In this way, you will not do this concealed thing.

The second situation: "You think you have done something to punish someone, but you don't want anyone to know about it". When you are in this situation, you can simply apply the method of overcoming concealment and then apply the thoughts of true forgiveness etc. to jump out of the conviction mode.

The third situation: "in your relationships, someone around you asks you to do something for him......". In this situation, you can deal with it by inviting the Holy Spirit in co-ordination with the way to overcome concealment. I am going to illustrate this handling method by the example I have just stated, as follows:

Your family wants to travel abroad. Your wife wants to go to Germany, but your child wants to go to Japan. So, the two of them have divergence. At that time, your child secretly said to you, "Dad, book the ticket to Japan, do not tell my mother, it doesn't matter whether she will go". And your wife also secretly said to you, "Do not care about our child's request, listen to me, book the ticket to Germany". What do you do about it? Are you going to buy a plane ticket to Japan or Germany?

When this situation happens, you can combine overcoming concealment with inviting the Holy Spirit. You should say to your child, "I won't hide from your mother by buying a plane ticket to Japan. You should talk with your mother". Then you should say the same words to your wife: "I won't hide from your child by buying a plane ticket to Germany. You should talk with your child". It means you are not going to do anything to conceal, and those words indicate that you have jumped out of their conflict. At this time, you are out of the conflict, and then you can deal with the situation by the practice of inviting out the Holy Spirit illustrated in this part.

There is a saying in the world: "If you want to play a decent guy, you should hide information of both sides, if not, you simply expose information of both sides". However, this saying in the world cannot resist deliberation. Why do you have to hide information of both sides? That is because when you are involved in the conflict between others, you are certain that someone else's conception has a certain kind of error, and then you are certain that their conceptions will have some conflict when they are put together, which you don't want to face. So, you simply cut off their communication to avoid conflict. However, this practice directly reveals: 1. You still convict both sides. 2. You still believe in your own subjective judgment. 3. You still believe in your ability to resolve other people's conflicts. 4. You are still afraid of some sort of fantasized situation. So, when you are involved in someone else's conflict, why not jump out of it and hand it to the Holy Spirit?

The three situations above basically cover most of the concealments in the world. To implement the thought of overcoming concealment, you need to practice it in co-ordination with other miracle minds. Therefore, I suggest that you take good command of all the thinking patterns illustrated in previous parts in the first place, especially the practice illustrated in the previous part, before you practice overcoming concealment. Certainly, it won't be too hard for you to practice overcoming concealment if you can skillfully practice all the miracle minds illustrated above.

Finally, a few more statements on overcoming concealment:

1. The concealment of goodwill in the world can be done. For example, the family members of a terminally ill patient conceal his condition so that he does not despair.

2. The practice of overcoming concealment is not fully applicable to the field of work, because concealment in the field of work is sometimes a rigid professional rule.

3. For relatives and friends beyond your immediate family, if they ask you for some help, for example, they require you to do something for them, or they want to borrow money from you. At this time, you shall consult with your immediate family, especially your spouse, before taking actions, because that allows you to avoid concealment.

The message of the required readings is about to be completed. By the end of this part, I have finished the most common worries in the world and the thoughts of removing them. In the next part, I will illustrate the last two most common worries, that is, illness and death. This is the end of this part.

December 2017

9 Triumphing over Illness and Death

The content of this part is practical methods to triumph over illness and death. Before the illustration, I will firstly clarify what the world in front you is:

The world in front of you is really lifelike for you. It has well-proportioned objects, strange voices, bitter and sweet tastes, various smells, and you who live in it also have delicate physical feelings. Besides, everyone in the world also has different ideas and pursuits, so sometimes you have to admit that the world is real. And you might say, "I took a bite of ice cream and I felt so cool. Is ice cream fake? So how could the world be a dream?"

I'm sorry. The perception of the world as true is just a result of being taken in. To put it plainly in the case of eating ice cream: the cool feeling you get doesn't come from ice cream, or from your body, but from your sub-conscious projection. The principle of this projection is as follows: your sub-consciousness firstly projects three illusions: your body, ice cream, and the cool feeling. Then, your sub-consciousness gives meaning to each of these three illusions, and its form is as follows: when your body is touching ice cream, your sub-consciousness will project cool feeling for your self-consciousness to perceive. At that time, your self-consciousness will be certain that all three illusions are true, and your self-consciousness will also recognize itself as a body. This is the result of the sub-consciousness being integrated into and manipulating the self-consciousness. So, the intangible sub-consciousness not only projects things and body, but also designs and projects all the feelings of interaction between things and body. This is the fundamental means by which the sub-consciousness deceives the self-consciousness. So, however real and orderly this dreamland is, it is an illusion, and that is an unchangeable truth. Your belief that the world is true cannot compete with that truth, nor can your thoughts and actions change that truth.

Along the way of your pursuit of truth, the moment when you get affected with a disease, is when you are most likely to be deceived, or you are most likely to identify yourself as a physical body, because you will have to admit that you are a body living in the world because of the discomfort and pain of the body. Therefore, I will expound the root cause of the formation of illness and the basic methods of curing illness, so that you can clear up a relatively big obstacle for your course of spiritual practice.

Firstly, the root cause of forming illness is explained:

Illness is a form of self-punishment that is manifested by a sin in the sub-consciousness. (The sin is the result of your previous conviction of someone else or of yourself in the sub-consciousness. The forms of conviction include attack and counter-attack, sacrifice and punishment, hatred and revenge, and abandonment and concealment, etc.) Because your sub-consciousness is already integrated into your self-consciousness and has already affirmed that you are a body, the self-punishment of sins and guilt sometimes revolves around the body. At that time, you get sick. But sometimes that kind of self-punishment will revolve around the self-consciousness, and you will experience life's adversities. So, all the illness of the body and all the adversities of life are forms of punishment manifested by some sins in the sub-consciousness. Certainly, this illustration is only about physical illness, because the adversities of life have already been illustrated in the previous parts.

Here are two common illnesses for illustration:

1. I ate some dirty food during the day and had a stomachache at night.

2. I didn't pay attention when I went down the stairs just now. I sprained my foot, but there was no fracture. However, my ankle was swollen and painful.

These two types of illness are very common in the world. The first type corresponds to most illnesses in the world, and its connotation is "Because of that, I got that disease". The second type corresponds to physical ailments caused by external forces. So, what are the causes of these two illnesses?

1. I ate some dirty food during the day and had a stomachache at night. The cause of this illness is: because of some previous sin, your sub-consciousness first projects some dirty food and manipulates you to eat the food, and then your sub-consciousness projects a painful feeling for you and combines that feeling with your stomach; finally, your sub-consciousness also manipulates your mind to think: "eating dirty food into your body causes gastrointestinal inflammation, and causes the pain, so later I will pay more attention to health". Your sub-consciousness uses the illness to punish itself, but your self-consciousness doesn't know all that.

2. I didn't pay attention when I went down the stairs just now. I sprained my foot, but there was no fracture. However, my ankle was swollen and painful. The cause of this illness is also a previous guilt. Your sub-consciousness first controls your thinking and ignores the safety issue of going down the stairs, then you fell down because of carelessness. Then your sub-consciousness projects a change in your physical characteristics, namely, your ankle starts to get red and swollen. At the same time, your sub-consciousness projects a pain and combines the pain with the swollen part of your foot. In the end, your sub-consciousness will control your mind to think like this: "what a bad luck! I was careless, but the pain is killing me. Next time I go down the stairs, I must be careful".

The illustration of the above two illnesses represents all the connotations of the physical illness: the sub-consciousness will first project the cause of a certain illness because of some previous guilt (for example, eating dirty things or falling), then the sub-consciousness will project a result of being sick; finally the sub-consciousness will control your mind to connect cause and effect reasonably. And in this process, the sub-consciousness will ceaselessly project the change of some body function (such as the change of immunity, metabolism and the uncoordinated operation of various organs of the body, etc.) or projects the change of various external body characteristics (such as bleeding, inflammation, swelling and so on). At the same time, the sub-consciousness will ceaselessly project some pain to be combined with these "changes", then you will think you have got an illness.

As you can see from the above explanation, the root cause of illness is just some previous guilt in the sub-consciousness. Therefore, I will follow this root cause to illustrate the fundamental method and practical methods of healing illness.

I ate some dirty food during the day and had a stomachache at night. When you feel stomachache at night, you can practice the following thoughts over and over again:

1. I just ate some dirty food in my dream and felt the pain in my stomach in my dream. The world is just a dream. (Note: this practice is exactly true forgiveness. It can make the illness and the sub-consciousness meaningless first, and then you can move on to the second step.)

2. You should find a reference beside you, preferably a person, and then you can give him the idea of innocence, and then you continue to extend innocence to the whole world and all people. Certainly, if you are alone at home, you can directly think about the innocence of your neighbors or people on the street, and then extend that innocence to the whole world and to all people. (Note: this practice will make you a peaceful miracle mind first, and then your thoughts and beliefs will jump out of the perception that you are a body, and you will be able to separate yourself from the sub-consciousness, world, body, self-consciousness and illness.)

3. At the same time that you keep the second practice, you should think like this: "my current pain and the process of being sick is the result presented by some sin and guilt in the sub-consciousness, but the sub-consciousness and sin is illusory, so the process of getting ill that sin and guilt presents (the event of eating dirty food) and the result of illness is illusory. And at this moment, that is true for all the sick people in the world, so no one really gets sick". (Note: this practice focuses on binding sin to illness, and to the process of getting ill, and then applying true forgiveness to all of them. It also focuses on true forgiveness of all other people's illness and suffering. If you understand that the illness and pain

of others are illusion, then your illness and pain will be illusion. Then your mind and cognition will be more firmly integrated in miracle mind.

4. You can practice entrustment of fear and tell yourself, "even if the pain in my stomach doesn't get better for a long time, I accept it. I accept it. Because however long the pain and discomfort will last, it is just a fantasized situation for me, so I will accept it." (Note: the patients fears that his illness will not recover quickly, and the patient does not want to live in pain and discomfort for a long time. So, you need to accept all the situations you are afraid of and don't want to go through right now. Such practices will make you a fearless miracle mind, and then your cognition will get fully beyond the control of the sub-consciousness.

5. You need to think hard in the state of maintaining miracle mind. Who are you hating now? Who else do you want to attack (change)? To whom else have you sacrificed? Who else do you want to punish? And then you should think what fears do you have? Are you afraid of those situations, or those relationships? Then you should think whether you need to do some concealed things. Finally, you should think about what kind of person you want to be. What other illusory objects do you want to bind for a sense of self-existence and self-worth? Think about them! Once you have thought about them, you can practice true forgiveness and other miracle thoughts. (Note: if you can be alert and practice all the important miracle thoughts in the moment of illness, a large proportion of the guilt in your sub-consciousness will be melted away. This practice will be of great help to the recovery of illness. And this practice also shows that your daily practice in life is the fundamental method to preclude illness. So, the major method to triumph over illness is to practice these miracle thoughts in your life for a long time.

The above five practices are the fundamental methods to heal illness. The purpose is to dissolve the sub-consciousness and the guilt in sub-consciousness, because:

1. The sub-consciousness and sins emerge in an organic whole initially.

2. Sins are stored in the sub-consciousness.

3. The sub-consciousness has become the dreamt world and your life experiences in front of you.

4. The guilt and sins in the sub-consciousness can manifest physical illnesses for you to suffer.

So, if you want to cure illness fundamentally, you have to bind the illness to the whole world first, and then you have to forgive them in a batch, because either illness and the world become illusions together, or become genuine together; there is no room for compromise.

You can see from the above explanation that illness is just the result of guilt, so in real life, even if you practice these five thoughts when you are sick, you will not recover immediately, because the guilt in the sub-consciousness cannot be dissolved by you at once. According to the example, to be frank, stomachache is a result of guilt, and the swollen foot is also a result. These results are just a kind of punishment that has been manifested, so you can only practice these thoughts while enduring pain, then you might ease a bit of pain, or may reduce a lot of pain, or do not reduce any pain at all. Under these circumstances, you can practice the sixth approach: you can cure illness in a secular way.

6. If you get enterogastritis, you can take some medicine to cure it or go to the hospital for treatment. If you have sprained a foot, you can apply medication for relieving pain and swelling.

The sixth approach is the most common method of curing illness in the world. So, what does that mean? I am going to talk about this unequivocally.

Starting with sub-consciousness, your sub-consciousness gave meanings and attributes to everything after it had projected the world and body. At the same time, the sub-consciousness designed all the rules and feelings for the interaction between everything in the world and your body. For example, water could quench thirst, food could satisfy hunger, temperature change could affect the bodily feeling, eating, drinking, excretion and sleeping could guarantee the body's operations and metabolism, and so on. The rules included a mechanism: a certain kind of drug or medical treatment would cure a certain illness. According to this mechanism, the sub-conscious projection was ceaseless. On the one hand, the sub-consciousness would constantly project more and more new illnesses because of sins. On the other hand, the sub-consciousness would also constantly project drugs or medical treatments that could cure these illnesses, and these drugs and medical treatments are produced in the form of being discovered or invented by people. (This is the so-called medical progress) So, the interaction between illnesses and medicine was a trick made by the sub-consciousness. The connotation of this trick is that the sub-consciousness would not only project the illness that was harmful to the body. If it would only project pains, the self-consciousness would doubt this world, so it also projected many things beneficial to the body while projecting pains, so as to ensure that the self-consciousness would not doubt the world and would be full of hopes about the illusory world.

When you have understood this trick of the sub-consciousness, you certainly can use it to get benefits, which means that you can use drugs and medical treatment to cure the illness when you are sick. Because in the world, illness often gives you a state of insanity, and in this state, it is difficult for you to practice the first five thoughts. Therefore, you can use medical treatment to reduce your pain in the course of illness, and then you will get a saner state of mind. At that time, you can better practice the fundamental methods of healing illness. (Note: medical treatment is only an expedient for the cure of illness, because it neither dissolves sins in the sub-conscious, nor prevents the guilt from manifesting more illnesses, but it does cure your illness and restore your sanity. So, you need to use it, and such methods are given to you by your sub-consciousness, so you naturally take it.)

These are the actual ways of healing illnesses, and then I am going to talk about death. The illustration of healing illness is completed, so there is no need talking about death in detail. If you are able to practice all the miracle thinking in life (the thought system narrated in "A Course in Miracles"), sins within your sub-consciousness will melt away because of years of practices, so at the end of your life, the advent of death will surely be without great physical pains. That is to say, you are most likely to die without illness, or you will only feel pain that you are able to bear. That's all. Moreover, if you can practice all kinds of miracle mind for a long time, you will not only face death calmly, but also be able to wake up to your truth before death. Then, you will no longer need to listen to others to narrate what death is, because you will be fully aware of the fact that death does not exist.

In the end, some reminders will be made:

1. When you have been practicing miracle minds for a long time while you are ill, you are very likely to go through the situation that your illness will be completely cured by some good doctors or medicines. It is also an external reflection of the guilt being dissolved.

2. If you suffer from the so-called terminal illness in the world, you can also practice according to the explanation in this part, but the final result may be a miracle, or may not be, because it varies from person to person.

3. The thought system narrated in "A Course in Miracles" can directly heal all the mental diseases and hysteria in the world, but it requires you to learn and practice this thought system by yourself.

4. The third book "Love Has Forgotten No One" of the series "The Disappearance of the Universe" elaborates on many ways to keep your body healthy and heal illnesses. You can read it on your own.

5. Many of the chapters in the series "The Disappearance of the Universe" narrate the connotations and knowledge of death in detail, and if you want to know more about it, you can read them by yourself.

At the end of this part, I summarize the required readings: the required readings I narrate are basic "prescriptions" to heal "all troubles", and all the "prescriptions" come from "A Course in Miracles", thus, I suggest you to learn "A Course in Miracles", with "The Disappearance of the Universe" series and my narrations as assistance.

I have explained the core content of "A Course in Miracles" in simple language, and I hope these narrations can lead you to the right path of self-practice. That is my task, and I have two others: 1. simple annotations of "A Course in Miracles", you can find them in the website's special column; 2. Completion of the role of miracle spiritual healer, because this role can help people quickly resolve specific troubles in their lives. In the next part, I will talk about the spiritual journeys of the healers and the role of the healer for all people. This is the end of this part.

January 2018

10 Introduction of "We" and Our Function

Proceeding with the above part, this time, I will introduce the common spiritual experiences of spiritual healers of Miracles and the role of them for all people. This part was written from my perspective in August, 2018.

First of all, I would like to introduce myself in detail. My name is Chong Weiqiang. I was born in 1982, male, from Tianjin, China. Now, I live in Tianjin. I graduated from technical secondary school. I got married at the age of 26 and have a daughter.

I started to have access to Buddhism when I was 25 years old. During the three years of learning Buddhism, I prayed to Buddha and recited scriptures every day. At that time, I had a simple understanding of Buddhism, thinking that learning Buddhism could help others and make my life better. However, I found that my life had not been as good as before since learning Buddhism, and my troubles were more. Moreover, I also found that many Buddhist theories could not solve specific problems in life, so I gave up Buddhism after I had underwent a series of pain and adversity.

Soon after I gave up Buddhism, my family members were led by friends to learn Christianity, and they began to urge me to learn Christianity and ask me to pray together. I thought it would be good to have a religion, just pray! So, I started my two-year study of Christianity.

During the process of learning Christianity, there were some doctrines that attracted my attention. For example, love can dissolve sins and pains. And another example, the coming of God is love. Moreover, there was another doctrine, saying: How you treat others determines how others treat you. When I heard these doctrines, I was happy, because I was a common person, and I had spent half of my life seeing all the pains and struggles in the world, so I especially hoped to find some way to help others out of pain. After hearing these doctrines, I practiced these doctrines seriously in my life. At that time, I was completely kind to others besides praying for others, so that I could help others when they were in trouble, and helped them at all costs. Because I believe in these doctrines and believe that others will change because of my efforts.

However, it turned out to be cruel. After I did many things to treat others kindly, I found that none of them changed at all. Later, the more I contribute, the more people got unchanged. At last, this kind of mental torture went beyond the ultimate limit I could bear. One night, I was totally angry and lost due to some things. Then, I recognized that these doctrines were fundamentally wrong, and there was no god who could speak those words. "God" is dead; there is no hope. Then, I spent the night in this anger and loss, and made a decision, "I will not study Christianity any longer because its doctrines are wrong, and I will not care whether other people change or not; I just have to be kind to them. I accept it". In this way, I gave up the study of Christianity. However, at that time, I did not give up the determination to pursue love.

Later, I learned about many other religions, including Islam, Taoism, Hinduism and so on. Then, I found that all religions concerned love, and there was something wrong with the doctrines of these religions. So, at that time, a decision came into my mind, "I won't rely on any religion anymore, and there must be another way. I'm going to find that way with my own efforts".

In the six months since this idea came into being, except for work and life, I had been thinking about what truth really is, what love is, and how to get love. In this way, during this period, I often felt "huge" light coming with me, and angels coming with me, and then I slowly felt that the world was an illusion created by love. However, after I gained this insight, a major myth arose in my mind. I really didn't understand why there was such a place as Hell. I didn't understand how love could create an everlasting hell of punishment (called Hades in China, 18 levels of Hell in Buddhism, fire lake Hell in the west). I thought, if love truly exists, everyone and the world were created by love, why did love create a hell to punish people?

As time went on, this myth became even more elusive in my mind. In order to find out the answer, I began to search online for some knowledge about "where people will go after death". On September 25, 2013, I saw a post in some post bar, which tells a case of how a hypnotist used hypnosis to cure mental diseases. (The hypnotist allowed the patient to see his or her reincarnation experience of last lifetime and earlier lifetimes during hypnosis, then the patient would be able to find some laws of causation between the previous lifetime and the current life, so that the patient can let go of something.) I read this post carefully because many of these cases narrate scenes after death. And then I see two questions and answers in the case. The hypnotist asked the patient, "Where did you go after your death? Would you go to a place you don't want to go to?" Under hypnosis, the patient replied, "I decide where to go when I die. I am not controlled by others". When I saw this, I knew there was no hell. Because the connotation of hell is that you are forced by legendary ghosts and monsters to go to a place you don't want to go to. However, the hypnotic told the truth, that no external force would interfere with a person after death, nor would he be taken away and punished by force. So, at that moment I was convinced that Hell didn't exist. And just at that moment, when the words "Hell does not exist" came into my mind, my mind was pulled by God to him in an instant, and I completely realized, "I'm just an eternal spirit created by God. I'm not a body. The universe also doesn't exist, but I haven't left God. I just had had a nap dream about my life within God". At this moment, I woke up.

After I experienced the awakening experience, I understood everything, but I don't know why I can wake up from the big dream of life. So I started buying books about awakening online and reading them. In the course of my crazy reading, I saw a book that mentioned "A Course in Miracles", and then I bought "A Course in Miracles" and started studying it immediately.

In the process of my study of "A Course in Miracles", I found that "A Course in Miracles" was different because I could see that the content was completely correct. However, I couldn't fully understand every word in the book. At this time, I had the will to figure out "A Course in Miracles". So, I began to study hard. Then, when I had read over 100 pages, I finally figured out why I woke up from my dreams. It turned out that my thoughts and actions from childhood to adulthood had completely fulfilled some of the important ideas presented in "A Course in Miracles", such as satisfying the genuine needs of others without expecting anything in return, forgiving everybody and everything in the past, and entrustment of fear, and so on. The content of "A Course in Miracles" has recounted my whole spiritual journey, and what it narrates are more than what I have ever experienced. Thus, in the course of reading "A Course in Miracles", I realized that the mission of my life was to practice and teach the book. Except that, I had no other mission.

In this way, I began to practice "A Course in Miracles", which lasted for 5 years. During these years, I studied and practiced "A Course in Miracles" for three times, wrote all the required readings and accepted the role of miracle spiritual therapist in 2018.

Those are my brief experiences. Here are two more awakeners I know well.

Pan Jinrong, born in 1985, male, from Putian, China, is currently living in the city of Hegang. He graduated from university, with proficient English. After graduation, he started a business, engaged in the building materials industry, and finally moved with his family to Hegang to do tile business. He has a son and a daughter.

I came into contact with Buddhism and entered the field of practice in 2012. I withdrew from the religion after encountering bottlenecks, and practiced the method of 'turning mind around' and 'Sedona Method'. When I found that I had solved all the perplexities in life, and the issues of money, power, fame, and wealth, yet my heart was still upset. In May 2014, I got acquainted with Chong Weiqiang on the Internet and began to study "A Course in Miracles". Within a month, I had browsed through "A Course in Miracles" and learned, "I have the need to be unity with the root of life. Since the world can not satisfy me, there must be a sole reality. All that manifestations before my eyes can only be a driving force for me to find God's love". I woke up on July 5, 2014, and my inspiration was that the world was my projection, so the world didn't have to exist. There is no world before I was born, and no world after my death. Since there's no one else out there, what is the meaning of all those?

I had achieved many important ideas in "A Course in Miracles" in the past. I am an absolute partner of Chong Weiqiang in the field of spiritual practice. Although I don't have many writing missions, I will complete the coordination with him.

The third awakened one is Pan Jinrong's only disciple, but at present her mission is not clear, so she only introduces the brief spiritual journey of her mind:

When I was 32, I began to have contact with the practices of physical and spiritual teachings. At the age of 33, I had contact with "The Disappearance of the Universe". A month later, I knew Chong Weiqiang and some practitioners of 'A Course in Miracles'. Then, I began to practice true forgiveness in life and study "A Course in Miracles". It took me more than four years to study the text of the course for 5 times, and complete the workbook exercises for 1 time. I woke up on February 22, 2018. My awakening not only depends on learning courses, but also because I have had a cognizance since I was a child, that dead people are pure spirits, and their painful lives do not exist. Therefore, the inspiration of my final awakening is: I would like to go home with these dead spirits, and I would be unity with the source of life.

The above are the 3 profiles of me and the other two awakened ones I am familiar with. If there is the fourth one, the fifth one or more awakeners I am familiar with and willing to benefit sentient beings in the future, I will make a new introduction.

Next, I will narrate the role of the healer for all in plain language. First, you can see from all the required readings and "our" profiles that "we", the same as you, are ordinary people with both parents and children. "We" also have experienced the sufferings in the world and conflicts in interpersonal relations, so "we" are not significantly different from you in life experiences. However, "we" are a little different from you if you look at it from the perspective of time, that is, "One might learn the doctrine earlier than the other", since "we" have found the solutions to all the troubles and put them into practice ahead of you. So, with this difference, you can turn to "us" in hopelessness and despair, and tell "us" about unsolvable worries in life. Then naturally we will give you directions and tell you how to deal with them. If you follow "our" guidance at that time, you will not only achieve peace of mind quickly, but also get the side benefits: transforming your destiny and weathering adversities in life. This is the primary role of the spiritual healer for everyone.

At the end of this part, I would like to thank some people, because without them, the role of the miracle healer would not appear.

I would like to thank to all the founding pioneers of psychic imparting and publishing "A Course in Miracles", I know four names: Helen Schucman, William N. Thetford, Kennith Wapnick, and Judy Whitson.

I would like to thank Gary R.Renard, the author of "The Disappearance of the Universe" and his assistant Cindy Renard.

I would like to thank the translators who translated "A Course in Miracles" into different languages.

I would thank the author Robert Skutch who wrote and published "Journey Without Distance".

Thanks to these people's dedication, the peace and light of heaven can enter the world smoothly. Because of their dedication, the role of Miracle healers emerges. Some of these people have successfully completed the task of bringing benefits to all people, and some are in the process of completion. So, I want to show that gratitude.

All major parts of required readings have been completed.

August 2018

11 Appendix I to the Required Readings: Work and Miracles

In this part, I will talk about the connotation of the field of work in the world and the fusion point of these connotations and miracle minds. The reason for me to illustration this part is that people often have troubles and confusion in the field of work.

First of all, I will narrate the main implications of all the work in the world: every work in the world has different pronoun, for example, restaurant cleaner, restaurant cook, restaurant boss, restaurant buyer and so on. These pronouns also represent different work properties, rules and techniques. And if these different rules and techniques are learned by someone, he would be able to do the work, and the job would bring him the corresponding monetary reward. And money can satisfy people's food, clothing, shelter and transportation. This is the main implications of the field of work in the world. So, whatever industry you are engaged in, you are restrained to the rules and techniques of your industry, but not restrained to any interpersonal relationships.

Here's a pretty straightforward analysis of the four kinds of work posts I've just listed, so you can see how to defuse the troubles at work.

1. Restaurant cleaner: if you work as a cleaner in a restaurant with 20 employees, you clean your area and keep it clean, then you get your work done, and you get paid. Other staffs don't make any sense for your work. Your boss, your leader, also has no specific meaning for your work, because your boss is a person who makes working rules and work instructions for you, so your boss only represents a set of work rules and instructions for you. This is your basic work connotations. It implies that you don't have any personal relationships with all the employees in the restaurant. So, you don't have to have a substantive conflict with anyone in your working field.

To put it more profoundly, this restaurant is empty for you, because this restaurant only has yourself, a set of work rules and a salary.

The only situation where you as a cleaner can have a conflict with someone else is that your boss may give you strict work instructions that make you feel like your pay isn't proportional to your salary when you are doing a specific job. Then, you can re-evaluate the return on your investment and salary, and then you can choose to keep working, or talk to your boss about salary raise, or find another job. This situation also tells you what kind of person your boss is, what kind of rule he represents, whether you can adapt to this rule depends on your choice. However, even that conflict isn't a real relationship conflict, because it is only what you give and what you get.

The work of cleaners explained above basically covers most of the work in the world. The work that is paid for with certain fixed rules completed belongs to the type of the work of cleaners. This kind of work is basically accountable. If there are mistakes in work, you should be responsible for them; if there is an error, you should correct it.

2. Restaurant Cook. This type of work belongs to the technical category. The connotation for this kind of work is not fundamentally different from that of cleaner. The only difference is that you need to use your expertise, which is the main source of salary, to complete work commands based on industry rules. If you are a restaurant cook, the restaurant only has you, a salary, cook standards you should follow and your cooking skills. Besides, the restaurant is empty for you.

The type of work that a restaurant cook does covers the world's technical and artistic types of work, which also follows responsible system and sometimes has more important responsibilities.

3. Restaurant Boss. The role has a complex set of working rules. If you are the owner of this restaurant, you not only need to set all the working rules for yourself and your subordinates, but also need to constantly give instructions for yourself and your subordinates. You not only need to follow the market rules and implicit rules of the restaurant industry to

keep pace with the times. You have to constantly train or arrange all of your employees to get to the right work post, because only by this will your restaurant normally operates. It doesn't matter who your employees are, in the process of fostering and arranging all your employees. What matters is that you choose the right person to follow your work instructions, which is what a restaurant boss is all about.

From the above connotation, you can see that the restaurant is also empty for you if you are the owner of the restaurant, because the restaurant only has yourself, the profits of the restaurant, and the rules of the restaurant owner that you should obey. So there is no need for you to have a real relationship conflict with restaurant employees.

Then, when you follow the rules of the restaurant boss, your restaurant may develop well, but it may close down. Because there is a saying in the world, "business is a battle, and it is natural for businessmen to gain and lose". It is possible to fail even if you do a good job to follow the above set of rules, which is nothing new, for there is no absolute thing in the field of work.

The above type of work done by restaurant boss covers most businessmen in the world and jobs with decision-making attributes. This type of work is more accountable.

The three jobs mentioned above basically cover the vast majority of the work fields in the world. You can see from the explanations in the work fields, everybody is responsible for his duty, rules prevail, rewards and punishments are clear, and survivors are the fittest, these laws are not negotiable. But the purpose of talking about those is not just illustrating the connotations of work. My key points are that there are no special relationships in the work area. There is no one else in your field because you face only a set of working rules and implicit rules. That's all. To put it more bluntly, you don't need to convict people in the work fields, or to form negative relationships in the work fields.

If you can understand this now and directly apply it to your work field, then you will be able to clearly recognize your position and role in the work field, and then you remove many worries in the work field. However, anyway, the human beings' ideology is not very advanced, social formation is also not very advanced, so the human beings cannot completely avoid forming negative relationships in the work field. Then, I will use a restaurant purchasing agent as an example to illustrate the situation in which it is easiest for negative states of interpersonal relationship to appear.

4. The restaurant purchasing agent: This type of work belongs to the business type and is directly linked to money. The connotation for this type of work is consistent with the three positions just illustrated. The restaurant purchasing agent also has a set of independent work rules. The purchasing agent only needs to follow these work rules and the instructions of the boss. But this type of work can easily lead to negative interpersonal relationships featuring concealment and fear. To put it bluntly, the purchasing agent may get the supplier's backhander after purchasing, and the buyer will never tell his boss about the backhander. At this time, the purchasing agent has built a negative relationship featuring concealment and fear with his boss. In other words, the purchasing agent has created a person making him fearful out of nowhere in addition to completing a set of work rules, that is, his boss. This is one of the most common negative relationships in the work field at present. This situation is also pervasive in many work fields. And sometimes you hide about something other than money, but whatever it is, if you conceal from and fear the other person in the work field, it means you have built negative relationships with other people in the work, unless your work rules involve confidentiality.

If you have these negative relationships featuring concealment and fear in your current work field, I suggest you learn the eighth part and then slowly practice in your work field to overcome this. I just suggest you practice slowly. This is the first time I use this phrase; because there are many hidden rules in the work fields in this age, people can't conquer the fear of money immediately, and there is also a kind of hidden rule like "if people do not raise the issue, officials do not investigate" in the world. So I just suggest that you take your time and practice being aboveboard in your work field. Certainly, if your concealment in the work field is against the law, it is rigid. Whether you are able to rein in on before it is too late is up to you.

The concealment and fear in the work field above is the first fusion point of the work field and the miracle mind. In the following, I will illustrate some other fusion points.

As for the second fusion point, we should trace back to the beginning of this part, "Work brings people money, and money provides people's food, clothing, shelter and transportation". This statement first represents the basic purpose of work. What is the purpose of food, clothing, shelter and transportation? The most basic reason is survival of the body. So what is the purpose of a person's body survival? Everyone has a different answer to this question. You might say, "For a better life, for better enjoyment of life." There is no problem for this answer, because no one is going to deprive your right to enjoy life. But I would like to sublimate your answer further, that is, the survival of body is the most important tool you can use to wake up from your big dream of life. You can only rely on a body to learn and practice this thought system that wakes you up from the big dreams of life, which is the ultimate purpose of body survival. If you are committed to this final goal, your attitude toward work, money and body will change dramatically, and your desire will decrease dramatically, which will play an important role in your spiritual cleansing.

All people living in the world have a deep belief in their sub-consciousness, that is, eating, drinking, and sleeping can keep the body running and alive. Although such a deep belief is illusory, it is difficult for people to overcome such an illusory belief in their big dream of life. What's more, a person's eating, drinking, and sleeping are independent events, which do not cause interpersonal conflicts or create sub-conscious sin and guilt. So you should make money in this big dream of life, and eat. You don't need to practice keeping your body alive without eating, drinking, and sleeping, which is extremely difficult to practice and meaningless.

As for the third fusion point, if you have practiced miracle mind in your life right now, you can practice the following miracle mind in your work field: you should listen to your co-workers' suggestions and reminders that conform to your work rules, and you can adopt them. As you practice this, you will find that every advice and reminder that follows the rules of the work can help you avoid many mistakes and troubles in your work field.

The above principle of miracle mind is relatively huge and abstract. You will gradually understand this principle in the process of learning and practicing the miracle mind. So I will just start with clarifying the methods and the benefits.

The fourth fusion point is the fusion of meeting the needs of your family and work field, that is, if your family just wants you to have a regular job, then you just need to meet the expectations of your family. Certainly, you can make more money on the basis of meeting your family's expectations, but your base line is to keep your family's expectations for your work. Because in the process of making money from your work, you sometimes impose what you think is the standard of happiness on your family, which generally means that you first decide how much money you need to earn to be happy, and then you think that your family thinks the same way. In the end, you completely ignore what your family really expects for you. Not only will you live a hard life, but your family will probably live a tiring life. At the end of the process, if you don't achieve the goal you set, there will be compunction and guilt in your heart, so this is not necessary for you.

The explanation of the above fusion point is the misunderstanding between work and life. So if you are already living in this misunderstanding, you can change your mind now. You can change your mind about the purpose of working and making money, making it closer to your family's needs and expectations.

There is also another misunderstanding that your family expects too much for your work, but you can't do it at all; at this time, your family may resent and attack you. When this happens, the first thing you need to do is to separate the public and the private mentally. Working and earning money belongs to official business, in which you should understand that you may not achieve the desired results even if you work hard, so the official business is out of your control and beyond the control of your family. After you have distinguished official business from personal hope, you can practice the thought of letting go of fear and punishment in the situation of resentment and being attacked. The results of this practice are unpredictable, but it is sure to be peaceful in the end.

The integration of the miracle mind and the work field has been basically completed. The original purpose of this part is to enable people to practice the miracle mind that wakes them up from dreams in a harmonious environment. And I hope you will wake up early from your big dream and fulfill your mission of benefiting all beings.

April 2018

12 Appendix II to the Required Readings: The Beginning of True Forgiveness and the Assistances for Spiritual Practices

This part of the message can be divided into two remarks from an experienced practitioner:

I illustrate the first remark with an instance: One day I broke a glass, and that affair was witnessed by a family member. Then the family member scolded me: "You are always that reckless. You have broken several glasses." What should I do at that time? At that time, first of all, I should realize that I was just scolded by a family member in a dream, and I should realize that the family member who scolded me was an illusory image that I had dreamed of. Then I could cognize that "the affair of breaking glasses and being scolded by a family member" just happened in a dream, and did not exist at all. Then I would realize that 'my family member' was just an innocent idea. At that time, the Holy Spirit would enter the relationship between me and the family member, because the Holy Spirit would perch within the innocence I had given. At last, the Holy Spirit would rectify some attack thought of my family member, and prompt him to stop attacking. That is the connotation of "To rectify others is not your responsibility, but the responsibility of the Holy Spirit".

It can be inferred from this example is that, provided that I apply the miracle mind first, the Holy Spirit will be invited out and bestow me a peaceful ending. The Holy Spirit is living within the mind of everybody, and always waiting for everybody to practice the miracle mind. The Holy Spirit is so close to you like that.

The second remark, what is the best assistance for spiritual practice? That is following the guidance of Arten and Pursah (Characters in 'The Disappearance of the Universe'), i.e., reading through the text and the 'manual for Teachers' of 'A Course in Miracles'(ACIM) every year, and complete the exercises of 'workbook for students' of ACIM every year. Certainly, sometimes the beginners will procrastinate for some time, so it is possible that you read through the text and the 'manual for Teachers' of 'A Course in Miracles'(ACIM) and complete the exercises of 'workbook for students' of ACIM in one and a half year. You are free to determine the speed, of course. But my experience is, if you can strictly follow the guidance of Arten and Pursah, the results you obtain will be the best. During the course of reading, you need to foster patience and perseverance. Because sometimes you will doze off in the process of reading, or simply fail to read on. Under that circumstance, if you can stick to reading the required part for the day by force even if you cannot understand it, your power of will is to grow, and the will to read and reading itself will become the most powerful assistance for your spiritual practices.

All The books I mentioned in the Tenth part are the gifts from the Holy Spirit, and they have the significance of teaching, especially the series of 'The Disappearance of the Universe'. Certainly, one of the books I mentioned was written by a human being. But many actual records in that book are also significant for teaching. For example, Helen Schucman dreamt a tome, then the Holy Spirit said, "It's time." Actually, You have also met that tome, and your time has come. There is also a scene described in that book, that the left side of the scroll is 'Past', and the right side of the scroll is 'Future', while in the middle of the scroll, there are two awesome big Words: 'God Is'.

Okay, this part of the message is short and simple, but it can well be the beginning of your spiritual practices, and I hope that you start your journey in miracles soon.

24 Feb 2019

13 Appendix III to Required Readings: Children's Education and Spiritual Practice

In this information, I will tell you how you, as a practitioner, shall think about children's education.

The reason for this information is that many people will forget how to educate their children because of their spiritual practices, or even worse, some people will apply the idea of spiritual practices to the issues of educating their children, and this blind application will cause some kind of conflict in their hearts. So the purpose of this information is to help you clarify the internal differences between spiritual practices and the education of children, so that you can greatly reduce conflicts.

First, let me define the attributes of juveniles in a broad sense. In the world, the group of juveniles is indeed a relatively "particular" group. Their "particularity" lies in the fact that the group will remain in a state of constant learning of the objective laws of the world. To put it in a simple way: a child from the moment of birth shall learn what to eat and drink, and then they have to learn what to wear as the temperature changes. And the commonality of these learning is around his body. That is to say, what a child should learn from birth is what is safe and favorable for his body, and what is dangerous and unfavorable. Then as they grow older, they have to constantly change their sense of self-identification and learn some general cultural knowledge. For example, he would be told by his parents: "You are a pupil now, you should do this and that. Now that you are a middle school student, you should do this and that. At this time, children will constantly change their self-identification. At the same time, in the process of growing up, children also need to learn some common legal rules and ways of dealing with the world. Until the end of the day, when he had learned most of the rules of the world, he would consider himself an adult. This is how children grow up. Of course, this process is what you have experienced.

From the above definition, you can see that in the process of growing up, children shall learn three categories of things:

1. How to make the body survive safely.
2. Basic cultural knowledge.
3. The legal rules in the world and the rule of universal interaction between people.

So as a parent, what you have to do is to educate and help your child learn these three categories well. This is not only your responsibility, but also something you have to do. Specifically:

1. You should teach your child what is favorable and safe for his/her body and what is harmful and dangerous. On this basis, you also have to do your duty to protect children. That is to say, when the child is in danger or will be in danger, you must be alert and protect his personal safety, and let the child get out of danger or avoid danger. You have to be as serious as possible on this issue.

2. As a parent, you should help and urge your children to learn "ordinary" cultural knowledge, which is also your responsibility. Notes in this article are: As a true practitioner, you should clearly recognize that every child's academic performance will not be the same, and the children's academic performance at each stage cannot be used as a criterion for the happiness and misfortune of children after adulthood. So you don't have to put undue pressure on your child's academic performance.

3. You need to teach your child the universal rules of interaction between people and some basic standards of good and evil in the world at the right time, and then you need to tell your child what bad acts are against the law. At this time, your child will gradually develop the correct legal concept.

To sum up, for a true practitioner, although the world is illusory, everyone is the son of God. But in linear time, your child is not a practitioner, and your child has not learned the universal objective laws of the dreamt world. Therefore, as a parent and practitioner, you should have a clear view of your child's education. You can't apply some ideas of spiritual practices directly to children's education in a confused way. Because if you do this, you will not only cause trouble for yourself, but also affect the growth of your children.

There is a rule in the world that everyone who comes to this world will first learn the universal rules of the world and do things accordingly, afterwards he will be able to enter the field of non-worldly practices. Therefore, it is your destined duty to teach children to learn most of the objective laws of the world, and learning these objective laws is the course that every child must go through, whether or not the child will enter the field of spiritual practices after adulthood.

Finally, if you want to ask what spiritual concepts are good for children? There is only honest quality and no concealment. You can teach your children to be honest with adults at the right time, or you can teach them not to hide things at the right time. The function of these two kinds of teachings is that it can help the child keep a smooth communication with you, and the smooth communication will help you to better guide the child, so that your child will not do something out of the ordinary. This is the key to parent-child relationship.

At the end of this piece I suggest that you should bind the "A Course in Miracles" and "Disappearance of Universe" series to read together when learning this information, because my information comes from both sets of books, and my information will not exceed these two sets of books. Amen.

Chong Weiqiang
28 April 2019

14 One-to-one spiritual healing rules

The healer will relieve your spiritual pain through one-to-one communication and help you get through life difficulties. As a help seeker, you first have to talk about your current adversity and your specific worries, and then you will get specific ways to remove them.

Before clarifying the rules, it is recommended that you read all the required readings on the website. Because you may be able to relieve yourself from the current annoyances and pain if you read all the required readings.

I would like to cite three guides from 'A Course in Miracles' as the foundation.

P-3.III.6. One rule should always be observed: No one should be turned away because he cannot pay.

P-3.III.2 There will be those of whom the Holy Spirit asks some payment for His purpose. There will be those from whom He does not ask. It should not be the therapist who makes these decisions.

P-3.III.6. Whoever comes has been sent. Perhaps he was sent to give his brother the money he needed. Both will be blessed thereby.

According to the above guides, four one-to-one healing rules are given as follows:

1. The healer will not refuse any genuine call for help, so you must come with specific questions and sincerity. There is no limit to the times of requests.

2. You should follow the schedule of the healer and the communication tools selected by the healer, including face-to-face communication, telephone, video chat, email and so on.

3. There is no rule of payment, and when the healer has finished assisting you, you may reward with money or give no reward. It is ok. It is up to you, and you decide how much money you reward.

4. If you just come to donate, you can simply say hello to the healer, and then the healer will say to you personally, "Brother, thanks for your hard work. Thank you for coming to support this cause that benefits all sentient beings.

To sum up, these four rules represent the word that the healer want to say to you, "the healer only demands your sincerity. Apart from the 'healing', there is no other thing relevant to him. Certainly, you may hide something in a one-to-one conversation, but this means you don't want to learn how to deal with it. So, I suggest you don't be afraid to confess to the healer, because the more you confess, the more you learn and the better the healing will be. There is a saying in the world, "Unsatisfactory things are common, and we just talk about a small part of them with others". The job of the healer is to relieve the pain that cannot be told.

If you want to find a healer for one-to-one communication, you can directly enter the one-to-one healing section of Road of Miracles Network for information query.

GENTLE AUXILIARY MATERIALS (PART II)

Psychic Work by Ann
(2017.11----2018.12)

1 There are countless bodies, but only one mind.

In 'A Course in Miracles', there is a saying: Because you think you are separated from the source that created you (God), you think you have committed a terrible crime against your source, and you can no longer be forgiven by him. Therefore, you can only bear this indelible charge and hide everywhere. Because the heart is so guilty that it cannot bear it, you use the creativity that He (Source, God) has given you to project sin on forms, that is, to transfer the sin that the mind thinks it has committed to the illusions that does not exist. Projecting what you don't want to face into seemingly realistic bodies that actually are mere images. You distinguish those bodies from yourself. You think that they have sins, and those sins have nothing to do with you!

You are trying to alleviate the guilt in your hearts in this way. In fact, your "Heart as One" knows that there is nothing except the Kingdom of Heaven of God. This deep memory cannot be erased due to the countless separate and seemingly real images you project!

In "A Course in Miracles", "Heart as One" is a very important insight that points to your true existence. There is no other heart, only one heart, there are countless bodies, but only one heart. Body is only an image created by the same heart to transfer the guilt. In this way, when the heart sends out any idea, because there is only one heart, so what gives and receives must be the same one. When you convict someone else, no one else actually accepts it. It's your own heart that accepts it. You are physically unrelated to other people, but in fact you share the same heart with them. As "A Course in Miracles" says, the other person's body you see is a projection of the same heart, and there is actually no other person.

Bodies do not really exist, just as you will have many shadows under many light sources. The shadows seem to be independent. They can be tall or short, fat or thin, with different postures, but they are all your shadows, all from you. All forms are shadows projected by the same heart, just that bodies seem more real than the shadows. In fact, they are essentially the same.

So the same heart gives and receives the same. When you see other bodies, the kind of judgment you make about them is actually the kind of judgment you are making about yourself. (How you perceive others, is how you perceive yourself) You can't stop thinking about right and wrong. In fact, the thought are all sent to you. Everything you create in your belief system is for you. What a heart builds is accepted by the same heart, there are no other receptors! Belief is what you send out, and it only works for you. All you build is yours.

2 Recognizing the untruthfulness of the world is the way to take you to the truth.

The channel through which my message is imparted is my spokesperson in the world. The wisdom of the message is received by you through the spokesperson of the channel. On your level, hearing the message is the most important thing. The message converts your belief system into a wise belief system, a belief system that takes you away from this dream, helps you recognize your dream and remember your real identity within this dream. As what the masters whom you know about have gone through, you can come out of your dream just like them. Only in this way can you free yourselves from all sufferings and truly experience happiness.

All sufferings come from the fact that the truth is basically completely forgotten. Dreams become your reality. When untruthfulness is taken seriously by you, you are deeply involved in it, and naturally the sufferings cannot be removed.

Therefore, the purpose of all methods of spiritual practice is to help you recognize that you are not the truth that you are deeply involved in and you assume in your mind, and that you are merely a dream that you have fabricated. Breaking this dream and leaving it is the only purpose of all the lives in the dream. (Here, I have a question in my mind: the real life is not in the dream, it is always in the kingdom of heaven. Answer: Please don't find fault with the choice of words. In fact, you are not in the dream, you just regard yourself as a person in the dream.) Therefore, it is necessary to recognize that you are not a person in the dream, you are not the body, and everything in your perception now. You are not anything in your dreams. Everything in your perception has nothing to do with your truth.

Truth cannot be perceived, so your perception has nothing in common with the truth. What you need to practice is to recognize that everything in the world is not real. To recognize that it is not real is the way to take you to the truth. In short, recognizing the untruthfulness of the world is what you are here for.

When you recognize that the world is not real, the world will disappear in your consciousness, and it can no longer restrict your freedom and happiness. Like the shadow you cast, no matter what it looks like, it won't affect you. Your freedom is released from your shadow. It is never able to limit your freedom. When you think of them as yourself, you will feel like you've lost your freedom. They have been given the magic (ability) to limit you. You are the sole restrictor of your freedom, and you are the sole master to release yourself. The Savior is nobody but you!

In the world, you can't wake up from the dreams you make, but it's an indisputable fact that you wake up in reality. You never leave the truth. How can you not wake up?

In your dream, as in your shadow, the shadow has no ability to recognize itself, but you can recognize that the shadow is not you, (just like) you can recognize that the body is not you. You recognize your dream in your reality. You can't recognize your dream in the dream. How can your body recognize that the body itself is not real? The body has no cognitive ability, the mind has cognitive ability.

In your life, you take everything seriously, and your feelings are constrained by the illusions everywhere, you cannot control your feelings, you are sometimes happy, and sometimes sad, and different reactions are generated vary according to whether you deem the illusion as beneficial. How can all illusions be harmful to you? How can your shadow affect your reality? How can you empower your shadow to determine yourself? But in fact, you have been manipulated by your shadow. Whether you want to continue to be manipulated by your shadow or to retrieve your true identity and rights, you are the decision maker.

3 Morbid beliefs and cognition are the root of diseases.

Hello, Dear Friends, Brothers.

Today I will talk to you about the problem of physical wealth that many of you are concerned about.

In your hearts, there is nothing more worrying about you than your body. After your food and clothing have been adequately guaranteed, your physical health has become the concern of many of you now.

Since the body represents you in your heart. Surely you see it as life itself, and try to make it live longer and longer, so that your life can last as long as possible in the illusion of time.

But the body is not the real you, you are the soul. The body is just a shadow projected by your mind. It is not the body itself that decides what it looks like, whether it is healthy or not. How can a shadow decide its own state? The form of shadow, its action, whether it is mobile or static, how can it decide by itself? You are the decider of all the states of your shadow. Like your shadow, the state of the body is determined not by itself, but by the mind projecting it. Therefore, everything that the body presents does not come from itself, but from the originator of the mind, that is, the cause of everything in the body.

Any state of the body at any level is determined by the mind, which is the cause. The sender, that is the cause, leads to the result, that is the body, is the law of cause and effect determined by Heaven, and this law cannot be reversed. The reversal of cause and effect is the root cause of all unresolved problems. The problem of the body does not come from the body itself and the interference of the external factors that you deem unhealthy. The only and fundamental reason is the problem of the mind.

Body is not just about the body you perceive, but about everything except the mind.

Body comes from the soul, expresses the soul and reflects the soul. The body is the most representative of the mind. The mind regards the body as itself. It is also easy to see the state of belief and consciousness of the mind through the health of the body. But a seemingly healthy body is not necessarily healthy, otherwise it will not suddenly die. (Here I thought to myself, some people are very healthy. The inner voice answered. 'A seemingly healthy body is not necessarily healthy. Otherwise, you won't die suddenly.') Every aspect of the body reflects every aspect of the mind. The blockage of the body reflects the blockage of the mind. The body is blocked at levels that your scientific instruments can't detect at all. In your concept, blockage at the higher level of the body is reflected in blockage at the lower level. For example, the blockage of meridians mentioned by traditional Chinese medicine is reflected in the obstruction of Qi and blood. The obstruction of Qi and blood, reflected in the solid level of the body, is reflected in pain, lumps and so on.

The body is the shadow of the soul after all. It comes from the soul and must depend on the soul. The source of physical diseases is the sick belief and cognition of the mind. The fundamental medicine for solving physical diseases is to correct the morbid beliefs and perceptions of the mind.

The so-called morbid beliefs and perceptions are based on the fundamental belief that the Lord no longer loves us, and that He has taken back all his love. I no longer have everything that He has given me, including perfect life. So I can't be perfect. The mind regards the body as himself, so none of the bodies He projects is perfect. The short life span of the body is the testimony of the mind that it is imperfect.

All the root causes of physical diseases lie in sending out the morbid beliefs and perceptions of the mind. The only cure is to correct the sick beliefs and perceptions. Correct them with mindfulness, that is to say, with the faith of the Holy Spirit as stated in 'A Course in Miracles'.

The faith of the Holy Spirit represents the message of God to the Son and the love of God for the Son. Trust in the Holy Spirit represents the message of God's love, that is, trust in God's love; that is, the correction of the sick beliefs and perceptions of the mind; that is, stop thinking that you have lost God's love; that is, stop thinking that you are no longer the perfect self created by God.

Trust in the Holy Spirit represents the message that the soul is willing to accept God's love, no longer shuts out the love that God has already given him, no longer regards him as an enemy to pursue him, no longer regards him as his own result; that is, to acknowledge that God is his own cause, and that he has always been the self that God created.

God is the cause, while oneself is the result. Just as one's mind is the cause, one's physical illness is the result.

Because the mind corrects the sick beliefs and perceptions, physical illness is cured and health is restored.

That's what we're going to talk about today, health.

4 Only that the body serves the mind means to be taken care of.

Hello, dear friends and brother:

Today I want to talk to you about body-related topics. The body is in a very important position in your mind. You think the body is your life itself.

The body shows its owner's identity everywhere. In your life, almost all the hard work takes place around your body. The body needs to eat, wear, live and travel, and the spiritual needs also revolve around the body. All hard work is around the body. The body becomes the master of the mind. The creativity of the mind serves the needs of the body. If you have a physical problem, you will be very nervous, as if your life is threatened.

You keep the body alive all the time. For example, you care about whether the body is warm or cold, hungry or full, whether it is recognized, whether it is respected, whether it feels valuable, whether it feels loved, whether it is in one body, whether it is caressed by another body, whether it has a partner, whether it is healthy, whether it has a big residence, whether it is in a comfortable environment, and so on.

You see, you are concerned with so many needs of the body, which makes you so busy that you don't have time to take into account your true identity, the mind. The body becomes your substitute, occupies your position, and you become its slave. When it fails to meet its needs, you are punished, and when it is slightly satisfied, you sneak a rest. The mind is used to serve the body, to serve a shadow, to revolve around the shadow, to take its own shadow as itself.

He who forgets that he has infinite power is like losing power.

You have a metaphor: "Asking for a meal with a golden bowl." You are beggars with golden rice bowls. I don't know that I already have infinite wealth. I have to go to ask for food and ask for alms. The Lord has given you everything you need. You don't remember begging for countless hours with a golden bowl.

In your begging career with a golden bowl, you dare not imagine: Is such a life wrong? Is it possible not to do so? Is there a better and easier way to be truly happy?

If you can stop often, ask yourself. That deeply buried memory, maybe a flash of light will pass. In this flash, something that has never happened in your begging seems to be awakened. Your life has opened a new horizon. Instead of repeating your previous life, you begin to look for the truth and find yourself. That's what many of you have begun to do.

Open new horizons, in your hearts, as darkness is illuminated by light. You begin to see the treasures that you already have, though vague, but at least you begin to doubt the life you have been living, and begin to look at the shadowy place that looks like treasure. Someday, you will find your own treasure and no need to beg. The body is no longer your master. You wake up from a dream of reversal of cause and effect. Re-establish your identity as the cause. Instead of revolving around the body, you use the body to create what you want and share what you are gradually aware of.

Identity is established, and in your mind you can use your body as a tool to walk in your dreams. Give it the necessary survival needs, but no longer be happy or sad, whether it meets the requirements of the labels stipulated to it in the dream, such as the labels of wealth, respect, beauty, and so on.

In this way, you are the real masters of your own, and you find their true identity, which is not far from home.

Physical care is not unnecessary. In this illusory world, the body is created according to certain procedures. What is set is that it needs energy supply and replenishment. If it's taken care of in this illusion, it's good for the soul to go on the journey home. The body is put in its proper place and can do what it is supposed to do.

The body does not need deliberate care, the soul is what you have to take care of deliberately. Always be aware of the state of the mind, discover in time its distorted state, and insane state, and correct it with the faith of the Holy Spirit. That's what you do every now and then.

5 Are you really happy in the world?

Hello, Dear Brothers and Friends.

The topic I want to talk to you today is: Are you really happy in the world?

Happiness is not unwanted for each of you. Of course, you say to yourself, I sometimes want to experience pain. That's because painful experiences can make relatively happy experiences happier. For example, when you are idle, you can't feel happiness without worrying about anything. You have to keep yourself busy and alive. After you are tired, you want to rest. You want to do nothing but rest. At this time, if you will get a rest, it will make you feel very happy.

You see you still want happiness, but you experience a little happiness by comparison. All the differences in the world will make you compare. In a better state, you feel a little bit happy. That's how you experience a little bit of happiness in this world.

Therefore, you are comparing, comparing, comparing vigorously. Without comparison, you can't even feel a little happiness. In the process of comparison, in order to obtain relatively good things, you are full of endless competition and endless labor. In order to get that little bit of happiness that results from comparison.

In your cognitive system, relatively speaking, what's beneficial to you, you think it's good. Relatively speaking, what is not beneficial to you is not good for you. The standard of goodness or badness is set up by you and is still changing. You are constantly struggling for ever-changing standard of benefits until you exhaust your last breath. You often say, as long as I have a breath, what will happen to me? But can you really be happy with these endless efforts? Does this endless effort really make you feel comfortable?

In the world, you seem to be alive, you are not living. You're treated as a machine, and you're constantly working hard until you can't move any more.

Is that what your life is like? Are you really satisfied with it? If you are really satisfied with such a life, why are you afraid and worried? Your fear and worry indicate that you are not satisfied with such a life. Because it's not the life you really want. What you really want, the world can't give you, because nothing in the world is real.

You can't find truth in this world, just as you can't catch the moon in the water. How can you find it when you're looking for it in a place where there is no reality? You try your best, only end up returning empty-handed, leaving only more fear and anxiety in your heart and more lack and discontent. To try to find reality where it is absent, you have been doing this all along. This is the evidence of your insanity, and this is the evidence that your heart has been deceived. You are deceived by the illusion, and you regard it as a treasure, fighting and robbing, and you have been playing a farce of contention. This will only make you feel more deprived and fearful. This will only make you more exhausted and dried up.

Truth can't be found in this world. Where is He? He lies where this world disappears. He will emerge when all illusions disappear. He is always there, but the illusory world blinds you so that you can't see him. Only when you no longer take this illusory world seriously, when you are no longer blinded by this illusion, only the heart that has got rid of dust can feel the reality.

The world is an illusory shadow. It never really exists. It is always the shadow of your spirit. The illusory world projected by the consciousness that are split from your spirit, constantly beclouds you. You are blinded by your shadow so that you cannot see truth.

In your guilty mind, you have created dreams full of fear everywhere. Your guilty mind projects its unbearable guilt and fear into the world. So how can you find happiness and peace in the world? How can this world of guilt and fear, which comes from your heart, bring you truth? The heart that has projected this world of guilt and fear, insanely continues to project fear and guilt into the world, and gets out of control. Because guilt cannot be dissolved, unsolvable guilt is the source of the existence of the world. Unless guilt is removed, the insane world full of guilt and fear will not melt away. When the world has melted away, the truth, which is always there, will appear. Truth is what you really want. Truth is what really makes you happy.

Truth is your real existence. You always exist because you are created that way. God created you. He created you according to His own truth. His truth is your truth. You are no different from him except that you cannot create you. He created you, and you are a part of his life. He made this assumption in order to ensure that you are always part of His life and that you enjoy all of him. This setting guarantees that you will always enjoy all of Him, which is the embodiment of His love. He is who you are. You are inseparable from Him and will always be so.

However, you forget all this, and you are filled with ecstasy by a crazy idea, thinking that you have betrayed God and that you have the ability to create yourself that is not created by God. All kinds of worries come from the crazy idea that you think you have become the self not created by God. The removal of this crazy idea is your salvation and the recalling of your reality. All your thoughts in this world are metamorphosized by this crazy idea. It's your journey home to get rid of all the ideas that come from this crazy idea. Because your crazy idea created the world and blindfolded your mind. To get rid of them is the journey to recall yourself.

However, it is not so easy in this illusory world. Thoughts are constantly projected from your mind, which requires you to practice your ability to perceive them. When they are perceived by you, you no longer allow them to act in a furtive way there. It's like seeing a burglar stealing and knowing that the burglar is going to move. What are you going to do at that time? Call the police. Who is the police? The Holy Spirit. Whether you can't call the Holy Spirit depends on whether you really want to catch the thieves. If you really want to catch the thieves, the Holy Spirit will definitely help you. If you don't really want to catch thieves, the Holy Spirit will not interfere with your free will. That's why distorted thoughts that you perceive can sometimes be reversed immediately, sometimes not.

In this world, the real does not exist at all, the physical world is like a shadow, it seems to exist, but doesn't really exists. You simply cannot get happiness from here. The happiness you think you get is just relatively less pain. Happiness can't be experienced in this world, happiness only exists in reality.

6 Are you really happy in the world? (2)

Hello, Dear Brothers and Friends.

Today we continue to talk about the topic "Are you really happy in the world?"

As mentioned in the previous passage, you can't find true happiness in this world, because this world is not real. The world, like your shadow, is the shadow projected by your heart. What can shadow bring to you? The existence of shadow depends on the material you bring to it. How can it provide you with anything in turn? How can it bring you happiness? How can it affect your happiness? It only seems to exist depending on you. You project yourself into a shadow. What shape it is depends on you, you are its decider, you are its master. What the world looks like is up to you, and everything it presents is up to you. Because it comes from you, can only exist because of you, it has no vitality.

You are often disturbed by the world and push the cause to the outside world. It really is: A pre-text for convicting somebody is never wanting. When you convict the world, you are actually convicting yourself. The world comes from you and follows you. You think the world is guilty. Aren't you saying that you are guilty? So you've always convicted yourself, it seems that you were convicting the world, but in fact you're convicting yourself. The world comes from you and must resemble you. If you can't get used to the world, you can't get used to yourself. If you hate the world, you hate yourself. You reject the world and you reject yourself. You made the world, the world didn't make you. You fabricated a world in which you can't be happy. Because happiness can't be in an unreal world. How can happiness be in the shadow? So you suffer in this world, because you can't forgive the world. You take the world seriously, set many charges against it, and do not love it. It's like your abandoned child struggling in pain. What you project comes from you. You project what you think you are into the world. Your projections are full of conflicts, wars, diseases, hatred, pollution, poverty, mutual distrust, mutual suspicion, unequal distribution and so on. All the situations you don't want to see come from you. You project yourself into the world, and the world you feel is you.

See if there are any of the things I listed above in your heart.

Do you have hate in your heart? Do you have a sense of deprivation in your heart? Do you treat everything equal in your heart? Do you feel hurt in your heart? Are there conflicts and contradictions in your mind? Do you feel that you are not pure enough? Do you feel inferior and ineligible to have good things? Are you in a pitiful state of mind? Do you feel inferior to others? Do you look down upon some people in your heart? Do you admire someone in your heart? Are there any people you cannot stand? Compare everything in your heart with the world and see if it's the same.

The world is the portrayal of your heart, and you decide what the world looks like, just as the shadow follows the movements of your body. The body decides the shadow, not the shadow decides the body. If we want to harmonize the movements of the shadow, we must harmonize the movements of the body. The harmony of the world depends on the harmony of your mind itself. Therefore, the heart is where you shall work hard, so the heart is the object you need to change. The mind is full of crazy and insane perceptions. How can he project a harmonious world? How can he create a harmonious figure for himself? How could he possibly not make the world crazy and messy? Only when he changes himself will his shadow change. Therefore, spiritual cleanliness is more important than any kind of work.

The mind has changed his crazy and distorted perception, and the world as his shadow is bound to change with it. However, from the point of view of a shadow, many people want the world to be a better place. At this level, it is in line with their level of awareness to tell them that changing the mind can change the world. From the perspective of truth, the only source of happiness, true happiness can only come from reality. Your truth is the Son of God, holy and perfect. Only when you recall your own reality can you feel real happiness. So how can you recall your truth? As

I said before, the reason why you can't remember your truth is that crazy and insane thoughts and perceptions prevent you from remembering your truth. The only way you can remember the truth is to stop your crazy and insane thoughts, stop believing that you are really separated from God, stop believing that you have betrayed God, and stop convicting yourself.

Likewise, whether you want to make the world a better place or to remember your own reality, you start with the change of your heart. There is no second way.

That's what I'm talking about with you today.

7 The Balance between the Law of the World and the Pursuit of Truth

Hello, Dear Brothers and Friends.

Today I want to talk to you about the right balance between the law of the world and the pursuit of truth.

The so-called law of the world here, I define it as: the law of life. That is, the moral norms you shall follow when you live in this world, which I refer to the connotation of the law of the world. Seeking the truth is the super-mundane law. This is my noun explanation that I have made.

Living in the world, we need to deal with people in our course of life. We need to be guided by the moral norms of this world and engage in the work and life of the world, and all the activities we carry out. Your collective consciousness regulates the unified standards in all fields. In life and work, you can't break away from a certain degree of limitations of these standards. Therefore, in the norms set by your collective consciousness, it is a practical issue to flexibly deal with the teaching of worldly law to you.

One of the important ideas of 'A Miracle in Courses' is that everything in the world is illusion, not real existence. How can we co-ordinate this important concept with the norms of the world?

Co-ordinate them in this way: the super-mundane law shall include the norms of the world.

Since everything in the world is not true, is it difficult for you to abide by it? Does obeying it deprive your mind of freedom? If you don't take it seriously, how can obeying it hinder your freedom of mind?

If obeying it affects your freedom of mind, do you really believe in the super-mundane law?

The super-mundane law includes all laws of the world. Because it doesn't take everything in the world as real. Therefore, there is no conflict between the super-mundane law and all the laws of the world.

Life in the world is more conducive to the realization of the super-mundane law. When all kinds of things in the world really can not affect your spiritual freedom, you witness the super-mundane law. If all kinds of things seem to have no hindrance to your spiritual freedom, do they really exist? What are they other than phantoms? They have been realized by you that they are not authentic.

This is the exposition of no conflict between the super-mundane law and the law of the world.

8 The Heart Is Your True Master

The heart is your true master. You have been taught to be your own master and not a slave. But you are always in the role of slaves, serving a shadow. You give up your sovereignty, your rights and your power to this shadowy world, to let it control your heart, to let it enslave your heart, to let it deceive and tease your heart. You have been crying out to be your masters, but in fact you are not your masters at all. But you think you are your masters. So, you never think about it. Am I my own master? Am I really a sovereign?

You think the world is a normal world, and the world should be like that. But this is a complete lie, a complete trick, a complete deception. So the real wise man is the one who no longer covets everything in the world and can let go of everything in the world. I don't mean to let you lose everything you have in this world; I mean to let it go in your heart. As for form, it doesn't matter whether you give it or keep it. It is you who no longer takes it seriously in your mind, are no longer enslaved by them, and no longer affect peace of your mind because of their gains and losses. This is what I call "letting go", and this is what I call "not greedy".

The world is but a dream. treasures, wealth and splendor are just matters in a flicker of the finger. The world is magnificent, rich, brilliant and huge, it is also an illusion. How can it be worthy of your glorious Son of God? It is not worthy of your identity as Son of God, but you think that it is all you deserve. You've worked hard, worked hard, and worked hard for everything you think you deserve. It's a hard struggle here. But all in all, it's just a dream. What you struggle for and earn is just a soap bubble. What are you fighting for? What are you wrestling for? What are you greedy for? What can't you let go? If you try to get happiness from this world, you can only catch the moon in the water, look at the flowers in the mirror, and seek fish from the trees. You will never achieve your goal. The world does not really exist, just as the moon in the water does not really exist. To get the moon, we need to go to its real place; to get happiness, we need to go to its real place, which is the choice of the wise, which is the choice of the truly wise, which is the choice of the person who has removed the barrier of ignorance.

You are afraid of losing the world, because you have no power in your heart, because you have lost the memory of God. When you can gradually cultivate faith in God through practices of true forgiveness and miracles, your greed for the world and your constant fear of the world will ease. The inner peace is much greater, the inner strength is greater, and the degree of external grasp is relaxed.

So what you have to do is not to grasp the world, but to build up confidence in God. The certainty that you believe in your identity as Son of God.

The source of your fear is that you believe that the world is real, that is, that you believe in your sins and that you are separated from God. No matter what kind of fear it is, what you think is big or small, whether you worry about yourself or others, its root lies in the fear that you think you have betrayed God. Ego can play tricks and design a lot of situations so that you can see fear and experience fear. But there's only one source of your fear, that is the perception that you have betrayed God deep in your heart. Through the practices of Miracles, you have completely reversed the root causes of all fears. If the root causes are removed, the seemingly diverse fears will be truly removed, and guilt will be truly dissolved, which is the fundamental way to solve the problem of your disengagement from reincarnation.

The reason why you are still afraid of the world and you are still worried that various bad things will happen is that you still take the world seriously. You still think that the world is your master, controlling your destiny and your feelings. You still put power in the world and fail to take it back into your own hands. When your heart is truly peaceful, the world that is the shadow reflected by your inner peace will be peaceful. You can't see all the unfortunate things that upset and depressed you in the past, because all the images projected from your peaceful heart are as peaceful as your heart.

The way to make the world a better place is to make your heart feel peaceful, beautiful, joyful and blessed. Your heart is free of fear and guilt. Like a flat river at the bottom, whose water is naturally flat. If the bottom of the river is uneven and there are cliffs, the river will not be calm. Whether your heart is peaceful or not reflects the outside world, just like whether the river is peaceful or unimpeded. It is futile to try to change the surface of the river. It is the bottom of the river, not the surface of the river, that is to be changed, if you want to make the surface of river smooth. Even if you take a lot of effort to level the river surface, it will soon return to its original state, because the bottom of the river has not changed.

The bottom of your heart is like a tortuous and uneven river, sometimes with deep ditches and sometimes with cliffs, so your emotions are full of ups and downs, so your world is full of contradictions and conflicts. Because the world is nothing but the shadow of your heart. Let your heart be peaceful! You don't have to change the world. Only when your heart becomes peaceful, like the bottom of the river is flat, the outside world will naturally be calm and peaceful.

9 How to Deal with Emotions

Emotions are signs in the body system that indicate whether you are safe or afraid, and who you choose to be in charge. To deal with emotional problems is not to deal with emotions, but to deal with who is in charge. When you are in a bad mood, it is the ego who is in charge of you. When you are in a peaceful mood, it is the Holy Spirit who is in charge of you. It is up to you to decide who is in charge. You are the master. It's entirely up to you to decide who will make decisions for you. You are the only person who has the choice between the Holy Spirit and the ego. The Holy Spirit and the ego need your authority to act for you. They act on your authority. If you delegate authority to the ego, the ego will react to things according to his set of thought system. If you delegate authority to the Holy Spirit, the Holy Spirit reacts to things according to his system of thought.

Emotions indicate the choices you make. When you empower the ego to be in charge, he sees things in a split way, he sees things in a frightened way, he sees things in an opposing way, and he sees things in a guilty way. What we see in such eyes must be attack, punishment and even destruction. Emotions will inevitably show the imbalance of uneasiness, fear and anxiety.

If the Holy Spirit is authorized by you, in the eyes of the Holy Spirit, everything is holy and perfect, everything is full of the love of God. Everything sends you a sign of love with the love God has given them. Nothing is not love, and the truth of nothing is not love. Within the sight of the Holy Spirit, the light of God's love shines. Within the sight of the Holy Spirit, peace, joy, happiness and freedom prevails as that within love of God. In the eyes of the Holy Spirit, the body is not real existence. The Holy Spirit sees the light of God from each body. No body exists. Behind each body is the integrated mind like a screen. The shape is just like the image on the screen. Below the image on the screen, which seems to be separated from each other, is actually always a whole screen that is not changed by the image on the screen. This is what the Holy Spirit sees. When the Holy Spirit is in charge, emotions are naturally peaceful and joyful.

Dealing with emotional problems is to deal with the question whom you choose, and who is in charge will have corresponding emotional indications. Who do you want to choose to be in charge? The Holy Spirit or the ego, the right of choice is up to you.

10 Other gods than God

Religion is believed by many people in the life you have lived through. All religions have their own gods to worship. Are they trustworthy? How can a man who knows the truth trust gods other than God? God represents the life of perfect oneness, which is the name of perfect oneness in human beings. If only the life of the perfect one is true, will other lives that do not belong to the perfect one be true? God and the perfect unified life that God create is the only being, those that do not share the same traits with him are not true. There is no substitute for the holy and perfect life. He can't be imperfect. What needs to be filled in? What else needs to be done besides him? Only imperfect things need to be worshipped and consecrated by organizations.

If you believe that the gods outside of you are gods other than you. According to the principle of spiritual projection, where are the gods outside of you? Is there really something out there that you don't have in your heart? If you don't have it in your heart, how can the outside world have it? God is you. You are God. The outer god you worship reflects your inner being. What kind of god you believe in, what kind of god you have inside. All the gods in religions you believe in are within you. You made them.

God did not entail your making. He created you. You made other gods you believed in. Unless you serve God wholeheartedly, you will serve the god you made. That God needs you to worship him just reflects your desire to be worshipped. You actually want to take the place of God and build yourself into a unique authority. People want to be a unique authority in their hearts, so they make many gods who only acknowledge their own authority.

In your life, whether it's someone you worship, or a god you worship in religion, or something you can't stop loving, such as jewelry, beauty, fun and delicacies, it's the god you made. You get happiness and satisfaction from these people and things, and testifies to your specialness and sense of existence through the gods you make.

God is the pronoun of what you desire in your heart. You yearn for God to fill you up. You forget that you are perfect. You belong only to God. You forget your truth and make a god in your mind to comfort your poor heart for the time being. The gods you make can only satisfy you for a short time, and you can return to a state of loss, because you can only get falsehood from the false gods. Look beyond God's creation and you're doomed to nothing. There is only one God, the perfect life created by God and His Son, and there is no other God.

11 The Topic of Projecting a Beautiful Dream

Dear brothers, you have learned that everything that seems to exist outside is only a projection of spiritual beliefs. The mind is like a film's negatives. The picture projected on the screen depends on the content of the film which has been taken long ago. The picture on the screen will never change until the content of the negatives has changed. Tragedy will not turn into comedy, war movies will not turn into warm and romantic love stories. Only by changing the content of the negatives, can the stories seen on the screen change. Therefore, the mind's negatives determine the dream of life. To change the dream of life is to change the content of the negatives of the mind.

Human consciousness is the negatives of the mind. Without changing human consciousness, the plot cannot change its content. The dream projected by the mind dominated by the split consciousness always shows such plots as conflict, war and grief. The dream projected by the Holy Spirit's integrated belief consciousness is the plot of friendship, peace and happiness, which is equivalent to a beautiful dream.

On Earth, the collective consciousness is dominated by the split ego consciousness, so the story of conflict, war and grief is constantly unfolding. Individuals, collectives, countries, the planet as a whole are such stories. In planets listed as of high evolutionary dimension in the dream, relatively, the main part of life is composed of belief of the Holy Spirit, so the plot projected is mainly about peace, happiness and beauty, with few conflicts. This is the dimension of many of you dream of, but it is still a dream. Relatively speaking, opposition, conflict and separation have dwindled a lot.

On Earth, brothers who have fewer conflicts of mind and forgive many guilts have experiences similar to those of the highly evolved dimensions. They experience few conflicts and antagonisms and most of the time, he experiences harmony, happiness and love. This has nothing to do with the dream projected by the collective consciousness of the Earth. He will not change his inner peace because of the living environment of the Earth projected by the serious conflicts and oppositions in other people's minds. The opposition of conflicts is not so experienced by him because of the external environment. He does not experience conflicts and oppositions because of such external environments. Because he has resolved many conflicts in his mind, he cannot feel opposition oppositions and conflicts. Although he is also in this dream, the dream he experiences is peaceful, his feeling is peaceful and joyful, his dream has actually been separated from the dream of conflict and opposition made by collective consciousness. His mind is no longer projecting nightmares, but relatively beautiful dreams. He does not experience a relatively beautiful dream because there is no apparent conflicts and oppositions in the world. Rather, he experiences a relatively joyous and happy dream. For others, things that cause strong anger have no effect on him and he is still peaceful. The nightmare for others is a blessed dream in peace for him. To be exact, nightmares lie in their own feelings. Those who feel auspicious and blessed have beautiful dreams and those who feel painful and uneasy dream of nightmares.

On journey recalling your truth, the scenery along the way will turn towards a better direction because of your constant forgiveness, which is an assured macro-trend. But it should be noted that it is not the beauty that makes your mind peaceful and happy, but your peaceful and joyous mind projects sceneries that makes you feel good. The good or the bad is totally a subjective feeling. Something you don't regard as bad may be an unfortunate thing in the eyes of others. The unfortunate things in the eyes of others may be far from unfortunate for you. Of course, collective consciousness plays an overall role in the environmental change. The world will become harmonious and conflicts will decrease because of the change of collective consciousness towards forgiveness and tolerance, which is the general trend. As far as individuals are concerned, they can make their own dreams, that is, dreams of peace, joy and good feelings, completely unaffected by the macro-environment projected by collective consciousness.

12 Life needs no skill, but forgiveness

Today's topic may be difficult for many of you to agree with. You have been taught many ways of dealing with people, such skills and methods emerge in an endless stream, and are constantly improving. However, more detailed and mature methods and techniques have no substantial help to improve interpersonal relationships. Skills and methods are not the fundamental way to solve interpersonal relationships. Improving interpersonal relationships and coordinating interpersonal relationships with people who are indispensable to your own lives depends not on the skills and methods of dealing with the world, but on "true forgiveness".

As we said earlier, the world is just an image projected by the mind. The people who appear in your life, especially those who are close to you, are the key projections that you can't let go of. In complex interpersonal relationships, the key people that affect your life are projected by you. They reflect the deep impression in your mind, or the "good" impression in your cognition, or the "bad" impression in your cognition. These imprints are the karma parts that you choose to focus on in this lifetime and need to be forgiven through the interaction of others you project with you. Of course, if you can't make good use of these interactions to forgive your guilt, these karma will not change and will continue to carry on into other reincarnations. So people appear in your life come to help you forgive yourself, especially those who are close to you. Among those close to you, the ones who hurt you is the first ones you should forgive. By doing so, you get rid of your sins and release yourself. Difficult interpersonal relationships are a great opportunity for you to forgive yourself. Those interpersonal relationships which are especially difficult to deal with, are hard to change fundamentally, if you don't apply true forgiveness. Skills and methods are not viable here. Even if some of them seem to be working, they are also the effect of your heart's inception to defuse guilt. So spend your time practicing true forgiveness. There is no more effective way to have the relationship you want than true forgiveness.

13 You Who Lost Your Own True Memory

Losing your true memory, you can only struggle with anxiety in the bitter dream you have made. Love has become an empty word that you often talk about, but you don't know true meaning of at all. What you call love is often just the exclusive right of the person or thing that meets your needs. Fear and uneasiness linger in your life, and the guilt that floats up all the time occupies your life. The unsettling things in your life occupy your consciousness, and they also occupy your dreams. Every moment, you are occupied by unsettling things. In such a state of life, you live like a prisoner. You don't know when you will be put on trial. You are always worried about the moment when you will be put on trial. You are always worried about the moment when you will be put on trial. You are just like a murdered prisoner who can't settle down for a moment. Your life is so trapped in the dungeon-like predicament of a wanted prisoner.

You may say, I still have happy moments. Yes, I can't deny you have time to be happy. The wanted offender has a little rest time, too. But even when you seem happy, there is a kind of hidden uneasiness that you may not notice, just as the wanted offender is uneasy even when he has a little rest.

This dreamlike theatre you built for yourself is so lifelike that you can't remember your reality. You can only regard it as your only home. Even though it is in ruins and full of conflicts, you have become a fugitive. You don't expect any good treatment. You are willing to be punished, because in your subconscious mind you actually remember that you have a very magnificent and indescribable home, but you destroyed it, you have no face to go back, no face to see the Heavenly Father who once gave you such a magnificent home. You are afraid of his punishment. You punish yourself. You decide that you are no longer worthy of the love of God. You decide that you will not be accepted by that magnificent home. You run away crazily from the place where you think you have caused trouble. This is your wandering journey.

You have been drowned in fear, you never dare to stop wandering to see if you really burned down the magnificent home, your extreme fear makes you dare not stop, afraid that if you run slowly, you may be caught up. You keep running and running and never stop to think about whether you really burned down your magnificent home.

In order to avert your 'crime', you disguise yourself as a person with almost no trace of your original face. You wish you had never existed before, so that the crime of seemingly destroying the kingdom of heaven would not fall on you. In order to clear up your accusation, you made the unique trick of denying your original appearance and would never remember it again, because that would remind you of the crime that you supposed you had committed. You suppose that if you forget yourself, you will bury all the crimes you think you have committed. You have been deceiving yourself in this way, and you have plunged yourself into the hell of the world that you can never escape.

Holy Son of God, wake up! This is not the real you who live a hard life. You are not in the hell dream you created. You just can't wake up. You always think that your dream is your reality, but it is not true. The real you are always with God and always live in the splendid and magnificent home of heaven.

Remembering your truth, you have not destroyed the kingdom of heaven, you have not betrayed God, and you have only made a nightmare in which you seem to betray the God.

14 'Sex' is Not the Best Experience.

Hello Brothers and Friends:

Sex is supposed to be the best human experience. The moment of orgasm is just a little bit of the feeling that the Heavenly Kingdom has "leaked" to the state of oneness in a dream. The "leakage" does not mean that the little dream has a trace of kingdom of heaven, but that you have only a little memory of the kingdom of heaven in your dream. The intercourse of the bodies reminds you of unified experience in memory. The body is regarded by you as yourself. The intercourse of the body is considered as the combination of the souls in your hearts. Deep in your hearts, the life in oneness that once existed is flashed by your memory. That is the deep psychology of sexual orgasm.

In the state of oneness, the climax of holy and perfect life of oneness is beyond your imagination. Some of you have the privilege of glimpsing the experience millions of times that of human orgasm, which is the language description of the perfect life in oneness. The orgasmic experience in the body level you yearn for is only one millionth of the dance of unified life, but you think that's the most wonderful experience you can get. When you really think you're happy, it's just a poor imitation of the kingdom of heaven. You are addicted to this inferior imitation, which can hardly be called an imitation. Don't you know that you are satisfied as beggars when you get a little bit of residual juice? All you want in the world is just something that seems valuable in garbage waste, but you have exhausted your life for that garbage waste, and made you live like beggars in your eyes. That's what your dream life is like, like beggars in your eyes.

Sons of the Divine God, you are the holy, perfect, abundant, eternal and infinite real life created by God. Nothing in the universe is worthy of you, just as the most wonderful orgasm you think is less than one millionth of your true beauty.

Please seriously consider what you really want. The treasure is not in this world. The real treasure is the kingdom of heaven. Your reality is the kingdom of heaven. Whether you want to put your confidence in reality or illusion, when you are sane, please make a choice, that is what you really want. Make a choice based on your true will, make a choice based on your sane true will.

Before recording this information, the channel (Ann) did a true prayer meditation. In the process of meditation, she enters an experience of slight contact with real life, that is, the deep consciousness of the heart is in a state of clearer memory of the real, and into a wonderful experience of transcending orgasm. In such a wonderful experience, she said from her heart to God: Dear God, you are my only true love, I love only you, I dedicate everything to you, let me completely melt in your life. Yes, it was her real choice. She experienced a satisfaction that nothing in the world could bring her and a wonderful feeling, which strengthened her real choice. She had already believed that God was her only true love and God was the only real one who could satisfy her. Through this experience, she paid less attention to the world and had more confidence in the kingdom of heaven.

Of course, through continuous forgiveness, she is more likely to enter such an experience. Practicing true forgiveness shortens her "distance" from the kingdom of heaven and makes her feel the "breath" of the kingdom of heaven more easily. Everyone can approach the kingdom of heaven and remember his truth through constant practice of true forgiveness. The most wonderful experience in the world for real life is nothing more than a poor and awkward imitation. Would you like to trade this imitation for your reality?

15 Why Mindfulness Heals Physical Diseases

In 'A Course in Miracles', it was said that the change of spiritual beliefs was the real occurrence of healing. That is to say, any healing effect on the tangible level is also the result of the change of spiritual beliefs. The real healing is to heal the heart, and the transformation of delusions of the heart into mindfulness is called healing.

At the level you are concerned with, you will not focus on the change of the mind, but on the change of the physical level, such as the formation of an organic lesion in a part of the body. You want it to become normal as soon as possible. Yes, you are concerned about this level. But organic lesion is only a symbol of your mind's sense of guilt. Illness does not occur in the physical level, but the illness in the mind causes the illness in the physical level. Based on this principle, only by changing the mind can the diseases on the physical level be cured.

To change your mind is to transform your belief that you are guilty, that you should be punished, into your belief that you are innocent and that you are always perfect. That's what 'A Course in Miracles' says, You think you're separated from God and deserve punishment for betraying God and committing an unforgivable sin. What is reflected on your body level is your punishing yourself with illness (apart from the individual who has gone beyond the heart of guilt and has to demonstrate it for the sake of teaching), which is the root cause of your illness. Change this insane idea and replace it with the mindfulness of the Holy Spirit, that is, you have never been separated from God, you have never betrayed him, you have always been inseparable from God, you have always loved him, God has always loved you, you have always been holy, perfect, pure and bright as the one that God created, and you are always with God in one heart and one life, so you don't have to punish yourself. By changing your mind's beliefs, the healed mind will naturally project a healthy body. This is a natural reflection of the relationship between cause and effect. The mind is the cause, the body is the result, the body reflects the mind, and the mind determines the body.

Consciousness of mindfulness emits a harmonious and orderly high-frequency fluctuation, which constantly changes the structure of what you 'particles', making them change step by step from the smallest structure that your physics classifies, to the macroscopic level, such as changes in atoms, molecules, cell composition, cell structure, and even to the level you can see. The diseased parts recovered.

This wave of mindfulness symbolizes the energy of love and love. Its source comes from God's love, and it is the symbol of God's love in the dream. The harmonious and orderly fluctuation of love makes the material particles reconstruct in a harmonious and orderly way. The above mentioned material levels reflected in the visible level of your naked eyes is health, that is, the structure and function of organizations and organs has restored orderly normalization. This is the general process by which the belief of mindfulness heals the body's diseases. Love is the only source of healing. 'Love' mentioned here refers to God's love. The Holy Spirit's mindfulness but reflects God's love.

16 True Forgiveness

Let me talk about the specific operation of true forgiveness. Of course, if you have a deep understanding of this right view, you do not have to follow this process step by step, but as a beginner, you are still advised to follow this process of true forgiveness step by step, which is more powerful for you to quickly and comprehensively understand this right view. Okay, let me give you an example to illustrate how to practice this true forgiveness. For example, if someone slanders you, frames you, abuses you, what should you do?

First of all, let yourself be quiet, quiet, remind yourself to be quiet, this quiet, is to let oneself no longer be led astray by inertia thinking and inertia responses. If you are not skilled in this exercise, you need to consciously remind yourself to be quiet, if you are skilled, the process may not be necessary for you. You can see immediately that the person who scolded you is not really there. But you are now beginners, so, because you are not skilled enough, you should remember to remind yourself, oh, quiet, quiet. This silence is to let you stop the habitual, un-conscious, and sub-conscious response to respond to him and refute him.

Well, calm down, then how should I look at this matter? Then I think of 'A Course in Miracles' teaching: this image does not really exist, there not really is such a person, such an image that cursed me there. Maybe if you really believe that this image does not exist, your heart may feel much better, much safer. However, often beginners cannot do this, it does not matter, you just stick to practice, the following process is to constantly strengthen the right knowledge and opinions, Initial, it can be difficult to achieve, and then it can be easier, and finally it is very easy to do and you can immediately do that.

I went on to talk about such a process of thinking. Well, the image I see is not true. There is no real person there to scold me. Well, but I do see one, one image. So, how does this image come about? Oh, "A Course in

Miracles" says that all images are projected from the mind, so this image is also projected from the mind. I am the cause of this image, this image is the result of my mind, my mind is the cause of this image, this image is the result of the projection of my mind. So, well, then, why does my mind project such an image? Oh, "A Miracle in Miracles" tells me that the image outside is the embodiment of my soul, that is, the film played by my soul, and that my mind's recognition is equivalent to the negative of the film. I see the image, just like the image I saw on the screen. The reason why I see a person cursing me there is that I cursed myself in my heart. I framed myself, attacked myself and was not satisfied with myself. I think I should curse myself in my heart, I think I am no good.

So why do I think so in my mind? "A Course in Miracles" tells me, oh, I thought I had betrayed God, I was no longer with God, I lost my original perfection, I was no longer perfect, and God was so good to me, gave me all the perfection, I betrayed him, I felt guilty. So, I will deny myself and attack myself. So, have I really betrayed God? "A Course in Miracles" tells me that, in fact, I did not really betray the Lord, I have always been with the Lord, I have always been perfect, we have always been the me that God created originally. So the thing that I think that I am separated from God and I betrayed God, "A Course in Miracles" says, it is not true, it is just a dream I made.

Then, the truth is that I have never betrayed God, and the split never happened, and the separation between heaven and man never happened. I am still perfect, I always own the love of God, since the cause of this split is not true, then the separate image I projected is not true. Then, I will forgive, if no one outside is there, I will forgive this brother, or what this person has not done. Of course, I also forgive myself for projecting this image, because the idea of splitting is not true, nor is the idea of splitting projecting this separate image true, nor am I splitting with God. I should forgive what I have not done, and I should forgive what my brothers outside have not done. That is to say, I can forgive because my brother didn't really attack me there and he wasn't really guilty.

155

I forgive me because I have not really betrayed the Lord. I have not done anything to betray the Lord. So I can forgive. This is true forgiveness. True forgiveness is because brothers, because I have not done anything, so I can forgive, it is not the same thing as what we usually say about forgiveness, we usually say that forgiveness, it is, first of all, to determine that he did that thing, but I am respectful, generous, as an adult, I do not remember little people's faults, I do not lower myself to the same level with him, I forgive him. This forgiveness is based on taking things seriously, and true forgiveness is not taking things seriously, because it never happened. Brothers are innocent, I have not betrayed God, I am innocent. So I can forgive. It's called true forgiveness.

Here we should pay attention to the fact that what we usually call forgiveness is essentially different from the true forgiveness prescribed in the "A Course in Miracles". One is not to care about it on the basis of that it is true. The other is not to take it seriously at all. I do not admit or believe that my brothers are guilty or that I have betrayed God. So I will forgive, so I will not blame my brothers and attack my brothers any more. I no longer complain about brothers, no longer hate brothers. So in fact, when you stop condemning this brother, hating him, complaining about him, you stop believing that you really betrayed the Lord, and you stop believing that you are guilty. Because, as we said before, you and your brothers share the same heart. The way you think of your brothers, is the way you think of yourself. When you don't think your brothers are guilty, you will no longer think you are guilty. When you no longer convict your brothers, you will no longer convict yourself. So when you forgive your brothers, you feel safe and comfortable because you don't condemn yourself any more.

Well, this forgiveness goes on, looking at the brothers from the perspective of life in oneness. You correct your delusions through the thinking you just had. You correct your delusions with the Holy Spirit's right view. You don't apply the pervious thinking of the ego to look at this matter anymore. You look at it with the right view given in "A Course in Miracles". So, you are thinking with the Holy Spirit, you are learning the Holy Spirit's right view, you are cultivating the Holy Spirit's right view, you are choosing to believe in the Holy Spirit, you are cultivating trust in the Holy Spirit, you are cultivating trust in the Kingdom of Heaven, you are in the process of remembering the Kingdom of Heaven.

When we say that the person does not exist, we should pay attention to the fact that "the person does not exist" refers to non-existence of the image, which is projected by the mind. This does not mean that the truth behind this image does not exist. To say that the image of the brother does not exist, does not mean that the brother does not exist, and that the brother is a son of God like you. Notice that the way you think about brothers will be the way you think about yourself. If you think that brothers do not exist, then you also think that you do not exist, but in fact what we mean by non-existence is that this image does not exist. Just as you are not this body, brothers are not bodies, but brothers exist, your truth really exists. What is the relationship between you and brothers? You and your brother share the same spirit. And to ponder it deeper, you and your brother are in oneness, you and your brother are the same God's Son, you and your brother and God are the same one.

So the next step in true forgiveness is to behold together with the Holy Spirit, which is called True Vision in "A Course in Miracles". That is to say, when you think in line with above steps, you think with the Holy Spirit, and then what? Look with the Holy Spirit on the basis of this thinking. The way you think will be the way you see, and how do you see this brother? First of all, you don't take this person, this body seriously. Then you need to look at him through his body, through this image, to see that he is the son of God, to see that he is innocent, that he is a part of God, and that part is actually the whole. Because there is no concept of time and space in the truth, and part and whole are only a description perceived in the mind. To say that you are identical with God means that you share the same characteristics with God. So, you own every characteristic of God, and there is no difference between you and God. Therefore, every brother is Son of God, but there is just one Son of God. Son of God is a part of God, but also the whole God, because fundamentally he and God is the same, integral, so he is part of God, but also the whole God.

Then finally, in your eyes, you can see with one of your inner true vision. Of course, first of all, you recognize in your mind that the brother I see is not the body, his truth is God, is the kingdom of heaven, is all, is complete and perfect. When you apply such thinking and true vision to think about him and see him, you are looking at yourself in this way, you will recognize your truth, or you are practicing to recognize your truth, you are the kingdom of heaven, you are the Lord, you are pure and perfect, you are infinite eternity.

This is the process of true forgiveness. Let's summarize it briefly. First of all, the first step is to remind ourselves that if someone curses us, slanders us, we shall remind us to calm down, calm down, and then what? The second step is to think with the Holy Spirit, according to the right view: oh, this is not true, this is only an image I projected, then why do I project such an image, projecting an image that someone scolded me, because I think in my mind that I am not good enough, I attack myself in my heart, slander myself. Why do I attack myself, slander myself, deny myself? Because I think I am separated from God, I betrayed God, I am no longer perfect.

So, have I ever betrayed God? The Holy Spirit has told me, the right view has told me, no, this is not true, then what is the true? The truth is that I am always with God, and I have never betrayed him. Well, since the projection is not true, then I have not really betrayed God, the separation between heaven and man has never happened. Naturally I shall forgive what this brother has not done. I also forgive the me that has projected the image. When you forgive the one outside, in fact, you forgive yourself, that is, you no longer take the idea of separation seriously, no longer take seriously the idea that have betrayed God, that is to dissolve the idea of separation.

The third step, further, or advanced true forgiveness, is to look with the Holy Spirit and see that the brothers are not this person or this image, but the perfect life of the unity with God, that is, God. You can say that he is a part of God, but this part is the whole. Brothers are the kingdom of heaven, the kingdom of heaven is God, the only perfect, pure, bright, eternal freedom, the only real life, when you look at brothers in this way, you are looking at yourself in this way, so by seeing the truth of brothers, you remember your own truth. That's why True Forgiveness can take you out of your illusions and remember the truth.

Of course, if you are skilled, you combine three steps into two. For example, you remind yourself to be quiet, be quiet, this may not be necessary, because you are very skilled, for example, you may reach such a level, oh, I see a person outside, cursing me there, or is not satisfied with me, blame me, then I immediately think, oh, the guilt within my mind has been activated, that is to say, I immediately see that my mind is still condemning myself and I still believe in the split heaven, from the image outside. Then, I immediately tell myself, the separation between heaven and man has never happened, I have always been innocent. Of course, at that time, you will naturally be able to forgive the brother outside, your heart knows that he did nothing, and that you forgive him is to forgive yourself, and he just come to remind you that you convict yourself again, that you still believe that the split really happened. Of course, this belief is wrong, and that is what the ego taught you. Then you can immediately replace what the ego teaches you with what the Holy Spirit teaches you. Then you can take the third step and see that this brother is not the body at all. You need to see the truth through his body. He is the infinite light, complete and perfect. Of course, this infinite light is not the reality of heaven. It is the closest symbol to reality in the illusion. When you can know this brother from your heart and imagine him as infinite light, then you will surely not complain about him and convict him.

Of course, there is more advanced forgiveness, all of the above need not be used. When you see a brother cursing and slandering you there, your immediate reaction is to laugh. I mean you can really laugh at it. In fact, your laughter is based on the previous constant practice, and continuous practice is that you are really able not to take it seriously, and you already know very firmly in your heart who you are, and you know that you are invulnerable. That's what the beginning of "A Course in Miracles "says, "Whatever is true, it's not threatened. Everything that is untrue does not exist at all." Although it seems that there is a person who scolds you there, you are not threatened because you don't take him seriously in your heart. You know exactly who you are and who he is. At that time, you don't need any defense. You will only live in a complete peace and a complete certainty of your truth. Eventually, Whatever is true, it's not threatened. The concept of threat will fade away in your mind when there is no real threat.

When you can reach such an understanding and state confronting all people and all things, you can live in joy and gratitude completely, because you really no longer identify with all images, you can really see through this image, and see the truth behind this image. At that moment, there is only the kingdom of heaven, only eternity, only God, only pure innocence, and perfection. Facing the only truth like this, your heart will be filled with gratitude, only joy. This is how you practice true forgiveness to a very advanced stage. You will often experience that nothing in the world can affect your peace, nothing in the world can affect your joy, nothing in the world can affect your gratitude. At that time, no matter what you face, you only have the feeling of peace and complete love.

Q & A OF MIRACLES (PART III)

1

Q: Why the Ego cannot win?

A: Ideas are inseparable from the source. There are two lines: the Ego thought system is inseparable from the subconscious, the subconscious is the source of the Ego; and the Holy Spirit thought system is inseparable from memory of the truth within you, that is, your memory of Heaven. Then the two lines will "fight" within your self-consciousness. So why can't the Ego win? This is because although your self-consciousness will be eroded by the ego, it will never be eroded to 100%. "The Disappearance of the Universe" once mentioned that Hitler was occupied by the ego to 99%, but he also kept 1% of memory of the truth so the truth memory that will not be totally lost is the reason why the Ego will not win.

"The Course in Miracles" is a course to train your self-consciousness to live again according to the Holy Spirit thought system. The practices of "The Course in Miracles" are also based on the memory of Heaven. So, "The Course in Miracles" is also a course that can expand your memory of Heaven. For example, when you expand the memory of Heaven from 20% to 90% through practices, you are very close to enlightenment, which does not entail 100%.

2

Q: How do you understand that "the real world" appears outside of the sub-conscious and can in turn purify the subconscious?

A: when you practice miracle minds, your spiritual experience will be independent of the subconscious, and will become a territory of its own. This territory is the unified and safe state of mind of miracles, and the emergence of this state of mind is based on true forgiveness (true forgiveness can dissolve the guilt and fear in the subconscious). So the state of mind of miracles or "the real world appears" outside of the sub-conscious and can in turn purify the subconscious. So the practice of being a miracle state of mind is the only way for you to correct all your mistakes and dissolve the current dream. Correcting mistakes doesn't mean you have to jump out of your self-consciousness first, then cancel your subconscious. The way to correct the mistaken route is to jump out of the control of the subconscious and become a miracle state of mind independent of the subconscious. Then your mind can stand on this foothold and return to dissolve all the guilt and fear in the subconscious and outside of the subconscious. This is the road map to fix the mind. In "the Course in Miracles", the state of mind of miracles is also called the vision of the Holy Spirit or the holy moment, and the peak of the state of mind of miracles is called "the real world".

3

Q: As for the so-called "true forgiveness changes the script", can it be understood as deleting the script of guilt and fear and adding a good script? Or switching into another script?

A: It will not add evil script, neither will it add good script. Miracle minds will only allow future scripts to constantly change (the constant arrival of peace) with the early arrival of awakening.

Q: The script has been determined. What does "determined" mean?

A: After practicing miracle minds, the script will change constantly, and then this constant change will eventually form a script. That is to say, if you practice miracle minds, it's one kind of script. If you don't practice, it's another kind of script. You can only choose one of them. And even if you practice miracle minds, there will be a third and a fourth kind of script in your future... Because when you practice very intensively or when you practice intermittently, you will create two different kinds of scripts respectively. However, no matter how many scripts you have in the future, you can only experience one of them. And the one you have experienced is just the one that is destined to happen, this is called "the script has been determined".

Q: So for those who don't practice, the script is very certain and unchangeable, right?

A: Yes, the script is relatively fixed for those who do not practice. However, his non-practice in this lifetime is also in his big script, because he will practice and wake up sooner or later.

4

Q: "The Disappearance of the Universe" says that the date of life and death has also been set. Does it mean that people's life span is certain? Pursah: "One day, as long as you find your own ability to choose, you will no longer be a robot. That is the big day when you declare independence." How do you understand the above passage?

A: For example, your husband scolds you and you fight back. At this point, you are a robot controlled by the mechanism of subconscious conviction. However, if you practice miracle minds, you know that he scolds you and grumbles about you, it's just the projection of guilt in your subconscious mind, which just happens in a dream and doesn't exist at all. At that time you can forgive him, and forgive him for scolding you, because there is no such thing. At this time, you will retrieve your own ability to choose, and you will be independent.

True forgiveness can change the time of death, but it takes exceptionally energetic practices of miracle minds. There are several things that are very difficult to change in the world: the period of death, your spouse, and how many children you have. But the very exquisite practice state can change these, only the very exquisite practice is not easy to achieve.

Q: It doesn't matter whether you change it or not when you practice exquisitely, does it? If it's really changed, will you know?

A: 1. Excellent practice can really lead to "you will think it doesn't matter whether the script is changed or not". 2. In the process of excellent practices, you can feel that you have changed a very difficult script. But the normal situation is that you can only feel the script has been changed once or twice in the process of excellent practices, and then you can't feel the "script change" later. This is because once you have confirmed perception, you will have absolute trust that miracle minds can change the nature of the script.

166

5

Q: "The Disappearance of the Universe" says, "From the perspective of illusion, there are indeed lives on other planets, and they have their own courses of forgiveness to take. They are also brothers of Christhood." I can't help but ask, "is there a forgiveness course in the animal world?" I also know that it's the ego's thought system that's doing the mischief, but I can't help it. How can I forgive when questions like this come to mind?

A: You can think that if you are human, you can ignore animal affairs. Because if you are as eternal as God, then it's not a question for you to consider whether animals can advance in spirituality or how they practice. And you're the only one reading "A Course in Miracles", you just need to practice the task in your interpersonal relationships. In "the Birth of the Course in Miracles", there is a saying: the right side of the scroll is the future, the left side is the past, and in the middle is "God is". One implicit meaning of this sentence is that you are the son of God who is one with the Lord and is eternal, and your left and right sides do not exist. So, how do animals in this world practice? Who will be the last enlightened person in this dream world? How will he wake up? Who is the first enlightened person in the world? In fact, you don't need to think about such questions. Because such questions do not exist for you, the eternal Son of God.

6

Q: What do you think of meditation, Mr. Zhong?

A: You can use meditation as an aid to practice, and then you can do it or not at will. Because meditation belongs to the practice completed alone, it does not involve the practice of interpersonal relationship. Meditation is relatively slow in the field of practice, and the text of "A Course in Miracle"also says: "you can meditate, but you may spend thousands of years to get enlightened through meditation." In fact, meditation is neither "safe" nor much slower than practicing miracle minds in interpersonal relationships. So I suggest you read Chapter 8 of the required readings, and then compare the solitude of meditation with the practicality of miracle minds.

A person's life can't be just for one person to practice, or a person's life can't always be alone. For example, an adult must have experienced the situation that you did something with a friend outside your family, and then your family knew about it. After knowing it, your mother had a view on it. Your father had a view, your wife scolded you, your mother-in-law hated you, and your father-in-law encouraged you. So, when you're in this complex environment, you say you meditate, is that possible? Your wife is mad at you, your father is hating your wife, and your mother is unhappy with your wife. Can you still have a meditative mood and environment?

7

Q: I want to ask you about eating vegetables or meat. Most of the time, my mind doesn't get tangled, but sometimes it gets tangled. For example, sometimes I want to eat meat, but I think it's good to be vegetarian. At that time, if I don't eat meat, my inner desire will not be satisfied. If I eat meat, I will feel guilty and other emotions. I feel that I have not controlled myself and indulged my desire, including some things that may worry about reincarnation. In this case, how do you train the mind to get peace?

A: The answer to this question is: it doesn't matter what you eat in a dream. It's not guilty of eating anything. But at present, there is no scientific and technological level of planting meat on the Earth, so you only need to do according to the objective laws of the Earth at present, that is to say, everyone eats meat, you eat meat, you follow the crowd. And you don't have to define yourself as a bad meat eater, because if you define yourself as a bad meat eater, it's not good for others to eat meat. So you can follow the crowd, and don't care about others.

The Earth is a very sinister planet, but being sinister is not a single blade sword, because being sinister can also mean that you can more easily break away from samsara. However, the key to liberation is not the relationship between people and animals, but the interpersonal relationship. So you just need to practice your interpersonal relationships in this dangerous place. You don't have to think too much about animals. And your relationships will keep you busy for the rest of your life.

To add another point, you can wake up when you practice intensively in interpersonal relationships. The universe seems very big, and the things in the universe seem infinite, but these things have little to do with your awakening, because your awakening depends on the people you meet in your life. Although your subconscious mind projects a huge universe, you have established interpersonal relationships with these people (up to thousands of people) in your life cycle.

8

Q: Since the universe is created by the subconscious, and the subconscious is deficient and fearful, it should have created what it has. Why can it create the way of nature? I have always thought that the laws of the universe are good, and the way is good.

A: To answer this question, first of all, we need to describe the heaven. 1. In the kingdom of heaven, you, Son of God, are one with God, and you are just an idea.

2. The idea of you realizes that you are the "center point" of Heaven (this is the meaning of the altar of truth).

3. You have an infinite number of Sons of God (ideas) that are integrated with you, and those Sons of God are also the "center points" of Heaven. So you and all sons of Gods have no possibility of translocation at all.

4. In the kingdom of Heaven, you will always realize that you are the whole kingdom of Heaven.

5. You will always realize that Heaven is eternal and infinitely large. 6. In the kingdom of Heaven, you will always realize that the kingdom of Heaven extends infinitely from the inner to the outer, but the kingdom of Heaven has no distinction between the inner and the outer, because there is nothing outside the kingdom of Heaven (this nothing is not total void or total emptiness).

7. There is no ideas of space and time, and there is no 360 degree spatial attribute.

So when you mistakenly think that you are leaving the Heaven and projecting the dream universe, you need to project a world completely opposite to the Heaven, because only in this way can you completely forget the Heaven and get rid of the fear of being chased by God. So, your subconscious mind projects translocation and 360 degrees of space, individuality, time, and so on, because these attributes are just the opposite of Heaven. Then there is another important attribute among the attributes of the kingdom of heaven, that is, eternity. So when you project the universe, you project the stages of "Becoming, enduring, decay and emptiness" instead of eternity, and the stages of "Becoming, enduring, decay and emptiness" generates all the natural laws, so the natural laws are not good.

So why is the subconscious so powerful? This is because you are extremely sacred, and you have the power to create (in the kingdom of Heaven, you and God have worked together to create an infinite number of spiritual power of unity). So you mistakenly think that after you leave the kingdom of Heaven, you will change your creative power into the ability of projection, and project an illusion opposite to the kingdom of Heaven in your dream.

Of course, you may not think you have such a great ability now, but sooner or later you will wake up from your dream. And when you wake up, you will naturally understand that projecting a universe is a small thing for your truth.

9

Q: Is the Way, the eternal Way and the laws of the universe the same thing?

A: There is a saying in Taoism called "one Yang and ten thousand Yin", which means only one Yang is true, and all the ten thousand Yin surrounding this Yang do not exist. This statement is left by an enlightened Taoist, who speaks the truth. And the Way you ask about, in view of the current era, is basically that immovable consciousness, that is, the very pure state before consciousness has yet become the subconscious (the water drop wanders and produces the pure consciousness in the first chapter of the required readings). This consciousness is also the truth of "Delicate True Mind" in the "Shurangama Sutra". When the truth of "Delicate True Mind" is restrained by fear, it becomes the mind of delusion (subconscious), and then the mind of delusion projects the world. So from my personal point of view, in the current era, Taoism's Way basically refers to that pure consciousness.

10

Q: Are all systems, all methods and all images in the world created by the great power of the God?

A: No. The power created by God will not appear in this dream world at all.

11

Q: Is the so-called Tao, emptiness, Nirvana silence, infinity and so on the first state of consciousness after the little water drops are wandering?

A: Nirvana silence is the word describing Heaven. So is infinity. But there is no Tao and emptiness in the kingdom of Heaven. Tao and emptiness belong to the level of illusion. For example, you can say that miraculous state of mind and the real world are peaceful, which is OK, but the kingdom of Heaven cannot be described by tranquility. Because the kingdom of Heaven is completely silent. Peace is not the same as silence.

Q: What's the point of staying in such a heaven?

A: The good feelings in Heaven are more than ten thousand times better than all the good feelings you can get in the world. But you've forgotten that. And there is a saying in the world: "there is only happiness that people cannot enjoy, while there is no suffering that people cannot endure." So the answer to this question is that one of the purposes of practice is to ceaselessly bring your mind close to the state of infinite well-being. And when your state of mind can withstand the state of Heaven, the God will pull your mind into his heavenly heart (awakening). On the contrary, if your state of mind is not able to bear the heavenly realm, God will not pull you, because if He pulls you in advance, you will be frightened by the heavenly realm of bliss. So God will neither cheat nor harm you.

Q: From the perspective of God, Is the number of the lifetimes of reincarnation before enlightening is insignificant, because they are all illusions anyway? Does it make much sense that you facilitate people's enlightening?

A: Yes, that's what God sees. Of course, God has sent the Holy Spirit who can absolutely awaken you. As for whether you are facilitating people's enlightening, the answer is that when you practice miracle minds by setting an example, you are doing it. So it's impossible for you not to facilitate people's enlightening, if you are practicing miracle minds.

12

Q: Are those so-called big wishes just a kind of psychological comfort before they live out miracle minds? Because, although I wish every day, but there are still troubles. I really wish to help others, but they may not change much.

A: Making a wish is useful for your own practice. It has little influence on others at the early stage, because in the early stage, practicing miracle minds by example is the behavior of universally facilitating sentient beings' enlightening.

When you help others sincerely, while people still do not make much change, that may involve your sacrifice. You can read Chapter 6 of the required readings more.

13

Q: Now I understand the meaning of "bite your teeth to forgive". It's really bite your teeth!

A: Yes, the first time you practice true forgiveness or the first several times you practice true forgiveness, you gnash your teeth. Because you have to endure the anger, and at the same time endeavor to forgive those who attack you and the incident you are attacked. For it just happens in a dream, so it doesn't exist at all.

Q: When I first read the third chapter of the required readings, I suddenly had the idea that if I kill someone, I will not feel guilty and fear at all. When I finish doing it, I will completely forget it. No matter whether I am brought to justice formally or not, will I still get peace at the inner level? It's mainly because I once listened to a teacher's audio. She said something about so-called karma. If you kill five people, and you forget all about it when you have done it, and you do not worry that others will find you for revenge, and do not worry about retribution, nothing will happen. What do you think of it?

A: when you read Chapter 5 of the required readings, you find annotation at the end of that chapter. Because you dream of a law that can imprison the body, you'd better follow the law. And your teacher's words are also very irresponsible, because if you kill people, your guilt will enter the subconscious, so you should not look for troubles.

Although fundamentally speaking, it's a dream if you kill someone and get shot or sentenced to life imprisonment, why don't you choose a better dream? How can you read in prison?

Therefore, it is suggested that you should not overestimate your mental state in the process of learning, nor think that the abandonment and forgetting in your mind can dissolve all kinds of guilt in your subconscious.

14

Q: In the dream, what is the relationship between each mind that dreams, is this dream a common dream? If a dreamer in a dream wakes up, what is his role in the dream? Are all the waking minds one mind? What is the relationship between mind and mind? What is the relationship between the awakened and the dreamer? In the dream, when a dreamer wakes up, is the dream still going on?

A: The question you asked is rather poor, but I know what you want to ask. Let me talk about it:

1. A subconscious is divided into countless self-consciousnesses, and countless self-consciousnesses bind countless bodies, and then countless bodies bind different lives. It also includes your self-consciousness bound body and your life. Finally, these different bodies and lives come together in a dream world. This is the nature of the world in front of you.

2. The person who wakes up is the one who gets rid of the dream. The person who wakes up seems to be the Holy Spirit. His task is to live the truth by example in the dream. From the perspective of "A Course in Miracles", the person who wakes up can not only practice miracles minds by example, but also share some experience or give others some guidance.

3. There is no such thing as "all awakened minds". When you wake up, you know what everyone is; when you wake up, you know that all peoples' minds are within one God. It's just in this dream that when you wake up, you are likely to help others wake up because of gratitude. And this kind of help is very unsatisfactory, because the person who wakes up knows that other people don't exist, but he has to tell these non-existent people the experience of breaking away from dreams. That's the meaning of what the Sutra says, "I bring all living beings to nirvana, but I know that there is nobody to enter into nirvana."

4. Fundamentally speaking, there is no difference between the awakened and the dreamer, because both the awakened and the dreamer are illusory. So the real relationship is the unity of the Sons of the God and the God and the Holy Spirit, and this relationship only exists in the kingdom of Heaven.

5. After a person wakes up from the dream, his dream will still exist for a period of time. This is the "Enlightenment period" mentioned in "The Disappearance of the Universe". But when he goes through the period of enlightenment and comes to the moment of abandoning his body, he will directly become the spirit of Heaven. And just at that moment, all infinite spirituality will be with him in the kingdom of Heaven. Then he will know that all dreams are over (including others' dreams). Of course, this is for the person who woke up, such as Jesus. For Jesus, who is now living in the kingdom of Heaven, all the sons are already in the kingdom of Heaven, and all the dreams have already passed.

Then this answer will lead to another question, that is, since Jesus already knows that all the Sons of God are in the kingdom of Heaven and all the dreams have passed, why does he write "A Course in Miracles"? This is because for Jesus and all the Sons, although the dream is over, the dream can be classified into "long ending time" and "short ending time". Generally speaking, although this dream only appears and disappears in a moment in your (the son of God's) consciousness of, it is full of long and short time in this moment. So in order to save the time that appeared in that moment, Jesus wrote a book called "A Course in Miracles", and let the book enter that moment, so that the time in the dream would be greatly shortened. So even though the dream is over for all the Sons of God, Jesus did that. And it's not just what Jesus does, because it's what you're doing right now. You, the son of God, are "practicing the life of miracle minds" in the dream, which is a "miraculous life" that you, the son of God, throw back to the past dream that has ended. And your "miracle life" will shorten everyone's waking time (in that moment). This pattern is the same as Jesus throwing back a "A Course in Miracles" to the "dream that is over".

15

Q: Is the Holy Spirit is our inner Buddha nature?

A: People who believe in Buddhism can understand it like that.

16

Q: Is there no difference in merits and virtue between the pure consciousness of the first separation and the kingdom of Heaven? There is a sense of eternity, peace and so on in both Heaven and the pure consciousness. Is that right?

A: Pure consciousness also belongs to the level of illusion, not the kingdom of Heaven. There is no merit and virtue in Heaven, so the merits and virtues in the world are also illusory. The representation of eternity and peace in Heaven in the world is the miraculous state of mind, and that kind of heartfelt feeling has nothing to do with consciousness (subconscious).

Q: Can true forgiveness and the methods in the required readings facilitate the unity with God?

A: The practice of true forgiveness and the methods in the required readings can facilitate the integration with the Holy Spirit and the miraculous state of mind; the peak state of miraculous state of mind is "the Real World", and then you will wake up in the Real World", and the awakening can be regarded as the integration with the God. You can read the first four chapters of the required readings more.

Q: Knowing that the world is a dream has enabled me to let go of a lot. I like to hear you tell the truth and break my persistence. What is true knowledge?

A: Everyone's way is different. I have also learned a lot of things, various things. Finally, I learned "A Course in Miracles", but "A Course in Miracles" is the most practical and thorough one.

Q: Is Jesus the little drop of water in the metaphor in Chapter one of required readings by you? Are we all small drops of water?

A: Yes. Jesus is also a little water drop. We are all small water drops, we are the same.

17

Q: One of the problems is that we habitually think in advance about things that have not yet happened in the future, and many times it's a negative assumption. It didn't happen, but when we think about it, we start to be afraid. Is this self-punishment? Is the illusion of time not broken?

A: What you said is the habitual fear, which is the fear of the future presented by the guilt in the subconscious, so you can deal with the fear with the methods in Chapter 4 of the required readings. The insight that "time is an illusion" requires years of miracle practices to acquire.

18

Q:What is the nature of God's love?

A: Practicing miracle minds in the dream world is the expression of the love of the Holy Spirit, which is most similar to the love of God.

Q: For thousands of years human beings transmigrate, Jesus also came, but the war never stopped. Does this mean that real peace can only be achieved in Heaven? Even if there are real saints in the world coming, the problem of war will never be solved at the phenomenal level. The illusion is doomed to be binary opposition?

A: If you are saved, the world will be saved.

19

Q: For the saying "all over the world" in Buddhism, my understanding used to be that Buddha nature can be reflected in all things. Now "A Course in Miracles" says that God does not know the world, "I" just use the infinite power that God endowed me to dream out the world. Can all things in the world be said to be essentially "me"?

A: You will brush your teeth when you wake up in the morning. When you brush your teeth, you can think about whether the toothbrush in front of you can be put into your dream last night? The answer is absolutely not. The toothbrush in front of you can't really be put into the dream you had last night. God is the same story. Like the toothbrush, the God will never enter your current dream.

Therefore, the essence of the world in front of you is nihility, and it will never become the real "you", and the real "you" can only be the Son of the God.

20

Q: When people are alive, this body is full of vitality, but why does the same body become a corpse after death? Who made him live, what did it lose that made it dead?

A: At the time of your death (under the condition that you have no enlightening experience in this life), your subconscious will simultaneously perform the following three manipulations. First, it will control your self-consciousness to come out of the body; second, it will project a soul entity and bind with your self-consciousness. Third, it will control your self-consciousness to think that you are dead and have become a soul entity. Finally, because of the belief "Becoming, enduring, decay and emptiness" that your subconscious holds, your subconscious will set that the body after your "death" will slowly decay and dissipate. So after you die, your body will slowly decay and dissipate.

21

Q: The body is like a mobile phone, computer and other terminals. The program is the script of different terminals, which are all set by the Ego. And "the real me" is the received signal, like the air wave that never disappears. If a signal regards itself as a terminal, it is ignorance. When it realizes that it is a signal, which never disappears and is omnipresent, and is not locked by the terminal, that is liberation. I wonder if this metaphor is appropriate.

A: I can understand you. However, it will be clearer if I change these words. Self-consciousness is like a mobile phone, computer and other terminals. The subconscious designs different programs and scripts for the terminal, which are all set by the Ego. And "the real me" has been sending signals to the terminal, like the air wave that will never disappears. If the terminal accepts the program of the Ego (subconscious), it is ignorance. But if the terminal accepts "the real me" 's air wave, it will realize its truth, and then the terminal will realize that it is not a self-consciousness, but a ubiquitous, never disappearing "real me", and then he will be free.

Of course, if you want to cross to the other side, you still need to rely on the miraculous state of mind. The world is so troublesome.

22

Q: Can you tell me more about the meaning of "the Enlightenment period" in "The Disappearance of the Universe"?

A: Yes, take Pursah in "The Disappearance of the Universe" as an example. After awakening, she experienced another 11 years of enlightenment period, and then she abandoned her body (bodily death) and returned to Heaven. So why do awakened people experience the period of enlightenment? There are two key reasons:

First, show gratitude to brothers. Because when a person wakes up, he will have such a clear cognition that he can't wake up without the illusory world and the brothers in the world. So the awakened person will have the desire of "I want to help those who have not awakened to wake up" because of the gratitude and the situation that many people have not awakened before him. At this time, the awakened one will embark on the path of sharing the experience of practice because of this desire. This is one of the reasons for the existence of "Enlightenment period".

Second, the person who has experienced awakening will be frightened to some extent if he is allowed to return to Heaven "immediately". Because the awakening experience is only the birth memory of the first son of God, that is to say, you will realize that you are the first and only son created by God at the moment of awakening, and there are no other sons in the kingdom of Heaven at that time. So awakening is just the birth memory of the "first" son of God. Then, when you experience this "memory", you will experience another period of adaptation in the world, because you will slowly realize that the real Heaven houses actually an infinite number of unified Sons of God in this period of adaptation. Then when you have this feeling, you will not be frightened by the scene of "infinite Sons of God in Heaven" when you return to Heaven. So if you wake up, you will not immediately return to Heaven.

You can also refer to a real case in 《The Lifetimes When Jesus and Buddha Knew Each Other: A History of Mighty Companions》: a seriously ill man wakes up a week before his death, and then he says to his wife, "the world is just a scam." This case shows that no matter how long you will experience the Enlightenment period, even in a few days, it will still exist. In 《The Lifetimes When Jesus and Buddha Knew Each Other: A History of Mighty Companions》, the awakened one will surely accept and recognize the existence of infinite Sons of God in the kingdom of Heaven in the next few days. Then he can return to the real Heaven in a peaceful and correct thinking and cognition.

23

Q: That is to say, through "A Course in Miracles", we are also cultivating a "sober" illusion, living in the illusion soberly. If we can live without a trace of restraint, when the time limit of the physical body is up, we don't need to package and reincarnate in the form of soul, that is to say, the awakening is complete. If you have any hesitation about the illusion, you have to pack it for reincarnation.

A: No. If you don't wake up in this lifetime, you will be reincarnated. The awakening experience must also occur when there is a body, and it lasts about 20 seconds. You can read 《The Lifetimes When Jesus and Buddha Knew Each Other: A History of Mighty Companions》 several times. It's very clear. 《The Lifetimes When Jesus and Buddha Knew Each Other: A History of Mighty Companions》 also emphasizes that awakening can only happen when there is a body, and it will never happen in the soul world after death.

Q: The experience of awakening happens when there is a body. When the body extinguishes, it will completely settle in Heaven, right? The guidance and transcendence of Bardo after death can enhance the situation of illusion, but it can't awaken. The above is my current understanding raised for discussion.

A: Yes. In the awakening experience, your mind will first be drawn into his heavenly mind by God, and at the same time, your mind will be transformed into spirituality. However, in the awakening experience, your thought consciousness will not disappear, because your thought consciousness will get a lot of confirmation in the awakening experience. For example, your mind will confirm in the awakening experience that you are the son of God, that the world does not exist, that reincarnation does not exist and so on. After many things have been confirmed, your spirit will once again transform into a mind and return to your body, and then the awakening experience is over. Of course, the awakening experience

190

does not cause any change in your appearance, because it only means that your mind has been reborn.

The enlightenment experience of Gary in "The Disappearance of the Universe" can't promote the word "confirmation", so everyone has to experience the "confirmation" of awakening.

Regarding the guidance and transcendence of Bardo: transcendence for the dead is useless for the dead. Because he (everyone) can only practice when he has a body. When he has no body, he is waiting for the state of reincarnation. Where he was born and his next life experience are all created by his life experience. So you can think of transcendence as a kind of caring funeral ceremony.

However, if you really practice true forgiveness and give innocence to the dead, it is of great use to the dead (forgiveness of the soul body of the dead does not exist and gives him the idea of innocence). Because this kind of practice can save the awakening time of the dead person (from the perspective in a broad sense and cross reincarnation).

The two worlds of life and death are just one dream, not two dreams, so true forgiveness and giving innocence can "Penetrate" the two worlds of life and death. Generally speaking, there is no boundary between the two worlds of life and death.

24

Q: There are two questions I would like to ask you for help. 1. A Christian told me on the way yesterday that there are actually two gods, one male God and one goddess. How do you understand this? 2. Why do some souls have been reincarnated for thousands of years and tens of thousands of years, and some souls have only been reincarnated for hundreds of years, and does the subconscious project countless individuals in an instant? Is there any subconscious in different periods?

A: 1. You don't need to pay attention to the saying of two gods. There are many practices in the world that can't even touch the side of truth. 2. At first, whether a subconscious split into many bodies at once, or whether a subconscious split into only one body and one self-consciousness, then split into two, two into four, and up to now, there have been countless body and countless self-consciousness, for those myths, you don't need to study too much. Because this history has nothing to do with your current practice. The world in front of you is like this at present, so you can practice "according to the present". About how it split at first? How about the form? What is the process like? These problems will not affect your current practice, and have little to do with your current practice. So in the required readings, I wrote the words "a subconscious can project an infinite number of bodies at once". The purpose of my writing is to match the current situation of the world, so that you can better practice according to "the present".

25

Q: Why are you alive? Is it to meet the needs of relatives?

A: One of the key objectives of practicing satisfying the sincere plea for help from others is that only when you interact with others can you define yourself by seeing what others are. This route is a practice process that you can't get around. So if you don't have this cultivation process and you just solely realize what you are, it may take you a lot of time to know who you are, or you can't find who you are at all. So finding out who you are is the key purpose of practicing meeting other people's sincere plea for help.

Q: "To live" is to remember and experience that you are "joy, freedom, love". It is very important for us to confirm that we are "abstract", which is the key point of our revision.

A: Yes, your task in the world is to remember your own truth, but the step of recalling your own truth is to see what others are before you can confirm what you are. But under what circumstances can you see what others are? It must be in interpersonal interaction, in plea for help from others, or in the common choice of you and others.

For example, my water heater is old. My wife is worried about leakage every day. She wants me to buy a new one. However, I don't want to buy a new one, because I don't want to spend money. I want to save for some time. Well, at this time, I will procrastinate with my wife and sometimes quarrel. At last, my wife and I cried out every day that she was afraid of being electrocuted. I saw that I couldn't delay, so I bought a new one. After I bought it, I thought: to make thousands of RMBs to fill the water heater deficit. Well, this is a very common set of ego thought and action. In this set of thought and action, although the water heater was purchased, I did not dissolve any deficiency, guilt and victim emotion in this incident. Then I will change a set of miracle minds and action to deal with this matter. My miracle minds and action are as follows: I will use the illusory money to satisfy my wife's illusory but sincere plea for help, so that my wife's fear can be dissolved. Then I will practice that I will not have any deficiency and fear because I am not bound with my deposit. In the end, I shall deem that the energy and time I spent buying water heaters are illusory, so I am willing to do it. Well, after I have practiced the above miracle minds and done the miracle action for the water heater event, although the water heater has also been purchased, my wife's deficiency, fear and the victim emotion that I may have will disappear. This is the difference between miracle minds and the Ego's thought system, and this difference is not the difference in the outcome in the illusory world, but the state and outcome of your mind being guided is different. One is being manipulated by the subconscious to continue to live vaguely in the dream, the other is jumping out of the subconscious control and integrated into the miraculous state of mind.

Q: The problem that has been puzzling me has been completely solved this time, that is, my family and I are very willing to help others, but why do they always quarrel? Now I found the reason.

A: Well, helping people with the Ego thought system and helping people with miracle minds are totally different stories. Because they lead you to different destinations. One leads to the continuous reincarnation, and the other leads to the end of spiritual practices: Heaven. What's more, miraculous state of mind can bring you peaceful situations continuously, and these situations can consolidate your will to practice, which is more powerful.

26

Q: It's not enough to see the body as a phantom. You have to give Brothers purity and innocence first, right, teacher?

A: Yes. Why Chapter 3 of the required readings bound to true forgiveness and the giving of innocence? It's because you see what other people are, and you become what they are. So if you only practice true forgiveness, your subconscious will define you and others as illusions and nonexistent, but at this time, you will be distorted. So when you practice true forgiveness, you have to give out purity and innocence, so that you can become pure innocence, so that you will not be distorted. So who is innocent? That must be the Son of God. That's why I'm solidly riveting true forgiveness with the first lesson of the Holy Spirit, which is giving out purity and innocence.

Q: The body is illusory, but the noumenon is spiritual and real. So if we only look at the body as a phantom and deny the existence of noumenon, then the noumenon is also denied. Is that so, teacher?

A: Yes. So the first step of your practice is true forgiveness, and the second step to follow closely is to see that others are pure and innocent, so that you will not deny the noumenon. Of course, this noumenon (miraculous state of mind) just resembles the kingdom of Heaven, it's just a raft that carry you to the other side.

27

Q: What is the overall structure of "A Course in Miracles"?

A: The structure of "A Course in Miracles" is: on the basis of telling you that you are the Son of God in a large scale, it uses a lot of ink to tell about the role of the spiritual thought system and all the tricks of the Ego. "A Course in Miracles" compares the result of miracle minds and the Ego thought system continuously, and the purpose of these narratives is to let you choose miracle minds automatically. This is the overall structure of "A Course in Miracles". Popularly put, "A Course in Miracles" tells you that there are two things between Heaven and you: one is the world projected by the subconscious and the set of thought system (the Ego) that takes the world seriously; the other is the miracle mind thought system and the miraculous state of mind to which that thought system leads you. You are free to choose which world and which thought system.

Q: When I encounter specific problems, sometimes I forget to practice true forgiveness and miracle minds. Is this normal?

A: This is normal. The normal process of practicing miracle minds is: when you are dealing with various problems, you will repeatedly jump around in two sets of thought systems. Sometimes when you jump to the Ego thought system, you will be unlucky. When you are unlucky, you will wake up and practice miraculous minds. This kind of back and forth jumping itself is a normal process of practice. And for beginners, procrastination of practices is also very normal. It's good to be able to practice, even if you procrastinate it a little bit.

28

Q: "A Course in Miracles" says that "what one owns" and "what one is "are the same thing. Teacher, what are "what one owns" and "what one is "? Can you delve into it?

A: For example, if you forgive someone opposing you, then when you forgive him, his body image will become an illusion to you. So when his body image becomes a phantom in your thought and cognition, your body image will also become a phantom. This is the reason why you will become the definition of the reference outside of you. Then, when the image of the person opposite you becomes illusory, there will be a vacancy in his image, and at this moment, there will also be a vacancy in your own illusory image. At this time, you can give the idea of innocence into the opposite person's vacancy. Then when you complete the above steps, you will find that the vacancy in you has been filled with the purity and innocence you have given out. At this time, your mind will experience purity and innocence. So this pure and innocent spiritual experience is an idea mentioned in "A Course in Miracles": "what you own" that you give out is the meaning and direction of "what you are".

29

Q: After reading your required readings and practicing for some days, I think I can understand "A Course in Miracles". Thank you, teacher!

A: No need for thanks. It is a task for me to write the required readings, and I am very relieved to finish the task. However, the required readings do have the following functions: ① the required readings are the practical narration of all the core concepts of "A Course in Miracles". ② these narratives can greatly reduce the difficulty of everyone's learning "A Course in Miracles". ③ these narratives can accelerate the advent of "the era of miracles". ④ these narratives can lead everyone to the right path of self-cultivation. ⑤ these narratives can shorten many people's lifetimes to be awakened to Self-nature. ⑥ these narratives can help all the masters of miracles in the future save a lot of teaching time, so that these masters will have more time to do one-to-one spiritual healing work. ⑦ these narratives can make those who "don't understand miracles and talk about miracles everyday" disappear gradually.

30

Q: How to forgive and deal with the worry of damage in reputation of people around me?

A: When the reputation of the people around you is damaged or other aspects are damaged, what you are afraid of is not what they have to lose, because you will worry about what you will lose "in a wide range", and the most direct expression of this worry is that you will be afraid of whether they will take it out on you and how they will take it out on you. For example, your mother gets angry at work, and then she goes home and starts to make trouble. At this time, of course, you can't help her solve the problems in her work, and if you attack and resist her, it doesn't work. So all you can do at this time is to forgive your mother and the fuss she make at home continuously. Because once you use miracle minds to deal with her family tyranny, the Holy Spirit will be called out by you, and then the Holy Spirit will help you to correct some of your mother's wrong thinking, and then you can really help her. Well, you can infer other things from one fact and think about it for yourself. Because there are so many things in the world that I can't talk about them all at once.

31

Q: Excuse me, sir. It says that Thomas was executed by the warlords when he was 36 when he went to India to preach. And Thaddaeus was gay. I suddenly felt that the disciples of Jesus were so unlucky. If I had practiced "A Course in Miracles", wouldn't I have become so unlucky?

A: Oh. Counting from when Jesus ascended to Heaven to the present, you have reincarnated for more than 20 lifetimes after Jesus' ascension. So do you think you have wasted those 20 lifetimes? How can it be? If you are now on the way of practicing miracle minds, it can be said that you have practiced and contributed to the truth in the past 20 lifetimes. What's more, now that we have entered the era of law, the past era of lawlessness is gone forever. So you don't have to think about that useless thing, you don't have to compare "your life" to "Jesus' time.".

32

Q: You wrote in the required readings that the subconscious manipulates us. I want to ask if the subconscious is controlled by the Holy Spirit. What is the relationship between the Holy Spirit and the subconscious at present?

A: The Holy Spirit does not control the subconscious, because the subconscious does not exist. The relationship between the Holy Spirit and the subconscious is that the Holy Spirit will turn the subconscious and the world it projects into tools that can make you return to Heaven.

Q: Which audience is "A Course in Miracles" for? Is it the Son of God (unified spirituality), the pure consciousness, the subconscious, the self-consciousness, the Ego, the decision maker, or the observer? Besides, who is practicing true forgiveness?

A: "The Course in Miracles" is about self-consciousness and letting it dissolve subconscious and self-consciousness, so self-consciousness can be called the decision maker. Then along the way of learning and practicing, your self-consciousness will feel that there is no self-consciousness and subconscious (including the world projected by the subconscious), and the only one that exists is the miraculous state of mind that closely resembles Heaven.

Q: Oh. That is to say, it is self-consciousness that initiates true forgiveness, and what feels the miraculous mental state of purity and innocence is the mind resembling the Holy Spirit. Is that right?

A: Yes. When you practice miracle minds, it's when your mind and the Holy Spirit are unified.

33

Q: Can the teacher talk about the fear of money? I always fear that when I am still alive, my money is gone.

A: Because a lot of your self-worth and sense of existence are tied to money, it needs a complex and long-term practicing process to overcome your fear about money. As for how to practice, the key issue is interpersonal relationship. Because most of the fear about money is bound to the interpersonal relationship in specific events, that is to say, although money is immobile, the people in the specific events that money finally binds are alive. Take me for example. My idea and experience of overcoming fear about money is that I always spend most of my money in interpersonal relationships to practice meeting the sincere plea for help from others. At last, these practices will turn into long-term peaceful situations, which also include my family's identification with my personality. Because my practices will make them feel that I have no deprivation and fear about money, they will think that I am a person who can bring them a sense of security. In the end, my family's fear about money will continue to decrease because of my practices.

So, how to spend money is the core of overcoming fear about money, not how to earn money. How to earn money is a public affair, and how to spend money is a matter involving interpersonal relations and private affairs. And the practices of miracle minds will certainly be carried out in the field of interpersonal relations and private affairs. So you can spend most of your money on your family and the relationships around you. In addition, other methods to overcome fear about money is not very useful, because everything shall revolve around your core interpersonal relationships, your trial is not "far away".

Finally, you should pay attention to one thing about the field of spending money, that is, when spending money for children, it may involve education, which is similar to work and business. So when you spend money for your children, you should be sober. Don't spoil your children too much (no matter whether they are adults or not). The money that should be spent shall be spent, while the money that should not be spent shall not be spent. In this way, you won't make serious mistakes in education, and your children won't suffer a lot in the future. This is a matter of attention in the field of spending money.

Q: My husband asked me to save money carefully. How can I practice?

A: He asked you to save more money, which is also his sincere plea for help, so you should save more money, which is also a kind of practice.

34

Q: Why is educating children similar to work?

A: Why is educating children a "job"? It's hard for me to make it clear in a few words, but you can think for yourself, are all the institutions that educate children in the world a kind of "business" institution? Then you can also think, whether your child is an object of education for you as his/her parent, even though you do not work in these "business" institutions? Think about these questions and you'll see why education is close to work.

Well, consider the above answers for yourself. Let me say a few more words. In Chapter 13 of the required readings, I also talked about some key points of educating children. Now I'll expand these points.

Take me for example, I pay great attention to the following two points in terms of educating children:

The first is to teach children to be honest. At the right time, I will instill in my children: "no matter how big a mistake you have made, as long as you tell me truthfully, nothing will happen, and even punishment will not come to you."

Second, I will teach my children not to hide. I will instill in my children: "before you do something, you should ask yourself, do you dare to tell mom and dad after you do it? Dare you tell Grandma or Grandpa? Dare you tell your teacher? If you think you dare tell these people, do it; but if you think you dare not tell these people, don't do it. " (children's version for "non-concealment")

So why should I pay attention to these two? This is because in this era, some children are either too independent or too domineering, and they are not easy to communicate with others. Therefore, as a parent, the first task is to establish a smooth communication with children, and the smooth communication can only be established on the basis of children's honesty and non-concealment, which is the "core technology" of educating children. So if you can master the "core technology", you can better control and guide children. It also allows you to use fewer punitive methods to educate your children. Finally, if you and your child can maintain a smooth communication, you may continue to suggest to your child: "I am an adult, I know better than you the standards of good and evil in the world, and I have more experience than you, so when you encounter a question you don't understand, you can ask me, and then I will tell you how to do the best, so you won't do wrong." That means you have mastered all the "core technology" to educate your child, and your child will suffer a lot less due to this "core technology".

35

Q: The article says that time is always holographic. According to the course, the past, present and future all happen at the same time. Can you illustrate to me with popular examples? I still don't quite understand.

A: For example, you are called Wang Wu in this lifetime, you were called Zhang San in your last lifetime, and you will be called Li Si in the next lifetime. Now, Wang Wu is chatting with Wechat. But at this moment, Zhang San is also living in his life and writing calligraphy. The same is true of Li Si, who is also living in his life and reading books. So you and Zhang San and Li Si are living at the same time. This is the popular meaning of holography.

Q: "I'm typing with Wechat now. Zhang San is also living in the present moment writing calligraphy. Li Si is also living in the next life reading books. These three "I"s are living at the same time." Excuse me, teacher, is this a parallel world? How do you understand this?

A: This is not a parallel world, and there is no parallel world for you at all. Because you have only one subconscious, and one subconscious can only project one dream world. However, in this only dream world, time is holographic, and the reincarnation of each of your lifetimes also happens at the same time. So linear time is basically a hoax. This scam also includes the time of this lifetime of yours, for example, your childhood and your present time also happen at the same time. Just because of manipulation by the subconscious, your self-consciousness can't perceive that time is holographic, which is the trick of the subconscious.

There is no time in Heaven, only eternity, so the world projected by the subconscious must be the opposite of the Heaven, so the subconscious projects time, and controls the self-consciousness to experience time, and then time becomes linear. This is actually a means for subconscious to deceive self-consciousness. Of course, this kind of deception is also a kind of self-deception for the subconscious.

36

Q: Can it be understood that practicing "A Course in Miracles" is also practicing in a dream? For those who don't practice, they have awakened in essence, but they don't know.

A: "The Course in Miracles" is a course practiced in dreams. On the issue of other people's awakening, you don't need to abruptly deem that all people have awakened, because the awakening experience is something that will happen in the level of illusion, and this thing also has sequence in illusion. So you can think of others as Sons of God who have never left heaven. At this time, you can completely distinguish whether others wake up (something unrelated to your practices) and how you see others (real practice).

37

Q: I just read a sentence in the text of "A Course in Miracles": "Please also remember that even if your invitation is only an understated gesture, the Holy Spirit will still respond with all its strength." This gives me great peace. My understanding is: for example, I'm afraid that my wallet will be stolen. When I read this fear, I realized this idea. Then I entrusted this idea to the Holy Spirit, and I knew that the Holy Spirit would help me. But when you just had a discussion with a practitioner, you replied, "When you are in fear, the Holy Spirit will not care about you. "It makes me feel unsafe. Is it that I when I am in fear, the Holy Spirit doesn't care about me, and I have nothing to resort to?

A: I'll tell you more about it. The meaning of "a gesture" in this article is: take the case of losing your wallet. When you are afraid, if you doubt a little about the situation of losing your wallet may also be a dream even if it happens, then that little doubt is called a slight gesture for the Holy Spirit, and then the Holy Spirit will intervene. Then your little doubt is likely to turn into a practice of confronting fear (entrustment) due to the intervention of the Holy Spirit. That is to say, you will practice once because of this doubt: my wallet being lost is also an illusory situation, I am not afraid to experience this illusory situation, and I will not be the victim of this situation. At this time, fear is far away from you. Of course, according to the laws of the world, you still have to put your wallet in place, and you can't be careless.

Q: I can understand that even a little question about this idea is an invitation.

A: Yes. Under the principle of true forgiveness, if you question the authenticity of an event a little, make a gesture to the Holy Spirit, and then the Holy Spirit will intervene. At this time, your "right doubt" will continue to grow, and it is likely to become a practice of miracle mind.

Q: Is this kind of appeal OK? For example, "I'm fed up. I don't want to take this anymore. I'm fed up. Holy Spirit, take it away for me."

A: It's not an appeal. It's a way to escape fear and push it into the subconscious. So it's impossible to resolve fear in this way, and the Holy Spirit will not intervene.

The minimum standard for calling on the Holy Spirit is: you can call on the Holy Spirit to help you see the unreal nature of the event and the world, or you can call on the Holy Spirit to give you some inspiration to help you see the unreal nature of the event and the world, which is the minimum standard for calling on the Holy Spirit.

38

Q: What is to love oneself, what is not to love oneself?

A: From the point of view of actual practice, not loving yourself is to identify a brother as a body and convict him. Because when you attack your brother, the subconscious, the world and sin come true for you, and you are hurting yourself.

To love yourself is to understand that you are the pure and innocent Son of God, and that other people are also the pure and innocent Son of God. Therefore, the principle of loving oneself is to love others as oneself, and the attribute of love must be an organic whole. Of course, the practice of loving oneself sometimes show up only when it collaborates with practices of various miracle minds.

39

Q: The last element of forgiveness is trust in the Holy Spirit and determination to rely on his power. Does trusting in the Holy Spirit and relying on his power mean relying on the power of the Holy Spirit under all the circumstances, or limited to interpersonal relations?

A: What this sentence means is that, please trust the thought system taught by the Holy Spirit and practice it well, because the thought system itself represents the power of the Holy Spirit, and the real you is the Christ who is integrated with the Holy Spirit. This is the meaning of this sentence. The reason why this sentence is called the last element of forgiveness is that this thought system of the Holy Spirit is based on true forgiveness.

Then, does everything depend on this thought system, or only in interpersonal relationships? This answer to this question entails your own learning and the accumulation of your own experience. But this thought system is really applicable to interpersonal relationships on a large scale.

40

Q: Can you explain the practice of "the Whole in Unity" of 《Love Has Forgotten No One》? The book says that Jesus practiced it.

A: Yes, the practice of "the Whole in Unity" originates from 《Love Has Forgotten No One》. This practice was actually practiced by Jesus all the time. But to illustrate this requires specific cases, so I will illustrate it with the example in Chapter 8 of the required readings. But when I've finished, please do not think this practice is easy. Because this practice is more suitable for those who have practiced the miracle minds painstakingly for several years in their lives.

In that example of Chapter 8, your father and your mother are quarreling about a matter. You watch them quarrel. At this time, you look around, you are surrounded by two people. At this time, you can practice "the Whole in Unity" on the basis of Chapter 8.

First of all, you can look at your father first. After you see him, you can think like this: my father's body is just a fantasy I dreamed of, which does not exist at all. At this time, his quarrel with my mother and their mutual conviction are just a dream of mine, which does not exist. In this way, it can be concluded that my mother's body image and the body image of all sentient beings in the world are false and nonexistent. And the dream world is just an illusory image of oneness, which has never existed.

Then you should continue to think: my father is just an abstract idea of innocence, and this idea of innocence will not be restrained by my father's illusory image, because the abstract innocence is beyond the body and will be extended infinitely. So my father's innocence has been extended to me and my mother, and this innocence will be further extended to the whole world and all sentient beings.

When you have completed the above exercises, your mind will not only experience that the unified purity and innocence have covered you and your mother, but also experience that the purity and innocence have covered the whole world and all sentient beings. And just at this time, your mind will feel that it has become that purity and innocence. At this time, you can complete half of "the Whole in Unity" practice. Because, in this specific event, you have two objects for practice. So at this time, you need to practice the thought a moment ago aiming at your mother once again. In this way, your practice of "the Whole in Unity" can be complete.

So at this time, you need to focus on your mother and practice your thought a moment ago once again: my mother's body is just a fantasy I dreamed of, which does not exist at all, and at this time, her quarrel with my father and the matter of mutual conviction is just a dream of mine, which does not exist. In this way, it can be concluded that my father's body image and the body image of all sentient beings in the world are false and nonexistent. And the dream world is just an illusory image of oneness, which has never existed.

Then: my mother is just an abstract idea of purity and innocence, and this idea of purity and innocence will not be restrained by my mother's illusory image, because the abstract purity and innocence is beyond the body and will be infinitely extended. So my mother's innocence has been extended to me and my father, and this innocence will be further extended to the whole world and all sentient beings.

At this point, when you finish the practices focusing on your father and mother respectively, the two innocent experiences that your mind has acquired (one for father and one for mother) will be combined. At this time, you have finished a practice of "the Whole in Unity". Of course, I'm not saying that there is any difference between these two pure and innocent spiritual experiences, because they are the same thing as each other in an organic whole.

Well, based on the above explanation, if you can practice against your father and your mother at the same time when they quarrel, that is to say, when they quarrel, you are able to think that the images of both of them and all the sentient beings in the world are illusions, and you are also able to think that they and all the sentient beings own the very and sole purity and innocence that is mutually contained, mutually integrated and extended infinitely. Therefore, the key point of practice of "the Whole in Unity" is whether you can forgive and acquit your objects and non-objects of practicing (all sentient beings) comprehensively and giving all of them innocence, when you encounter specific problems. If you can, then the unified purity and innocence you acquire by practice will become a natural state. At that time, it was impossible for your mind not to experience purity and innocence.

Of course, when encountering specific problems, you are likely to attach a lot of other miracle minds to practicing "the Whole in Unity". So I just said, "Please do not think that the practice of "the Whole in Unity" is easy to accomplish. Because in actual practice, it's very hard and uncommon for you to combine and practice miracle minds correctly according to specific events and characters, and this kind of uncommon practice is very likely to have made you "try your best". So it's even more difficult for you to carry on the practice of "the Whole in Unity" on that basis. That's why I say that the practice of "the Whole in Unity" is hard to accomplish.

Finally, "the Whole in Unity" refers to the natural purity and innocence, and refers to the pure and innocent spiritual experience that is mutually contained, mutually integrated and infinitely extended. This spiritual experience is called "the face of Christ" and "the Real World" in "A Course in Miracles".

41

Q: According to "A Course in Miracles", miracles can make people's perception leap from horizontal to vertical. How to understand "horizontal" and "vertical"?

A: The meaning of this sentence is that when you practice true forgiveness and give pure innocence in your interpersonal relationship, you are giving true forgiveness and pure innocence to other people horizontally, and this horizontal giving represents that you have first integrated with your brother in the purity and innocence. And just at this time, the Holy Spirit will directly enter into the unified purity and innocence, and your horizontal giving will directly become the vertical connection between you and the Holy Spirit (the Holy Spirit is the communication channel between you and God). Therefore, the moment when you practice miracle minds horizontally towards your brothers, the Holy Spirit and God will simultaneously and synchronously establish a vertical link with you. So it's much easier and faster to perform this practice than to grope for the truth. For example, meditation, sitting still and other ways are difficult to achieve your instantaneous connection with the Holy Spirit.

42

Q: In the face of people close to me, how can I forgive their past?

A: In the process of your cultivation, it is difficult to forgive the past of those close to you, especially those who are still around you at this moment. Because you will evaluate what they are going to do now based on what they have done in the past, and these things will make you a victim. Therefore, to forgive the past of a close person, you should take multi line operations: 1. Forgive the past of that person. 2. Lay down your past assessment of them. 3. Let go of all your current assessment of them. 4. Face what will happen by means of entrusting fear. 5. Consider whether what will happen is a sincere plea for help from the other party. If so, deal with it appropriately.

However, the above answers do not apply to the scope of educating children.

43

Q: Will you still be distracted after you have broken away from reincarnation? What if you dream again when you have gone back to Heaven?

A: To answer this question, first of all, we need to illustrate the relationship between truth and belief. The reason why truth is true is that truth is within you. Therefore, belief in truth cannot be confirmed by you or identified by you as proof through the description of someone outside of you. Because the answer is in you, you can only realize the truth is true. That is to say, you can only experience the truth that you are the Son of God and reside in Heaven through your own experience and final experience (this is an auxiliary answer).

Next, I will forcibly say the whole process of "things" in words:

"In the beginning", God created the only one you (Son of God) who lived in him. Then you and God create an infinite number of Sons of the God (that is the meaning that you are the co-creator of God), and the kingdom of Heaven is accomplished. So the "accomplished" Heaven is a state in which the infinite number of Sons of God are with God. That is to say, the "present" appearance of the kingdom of Heaven has gone beyond the "original" (in fact, there is no original) process that God created the only one you. Then because the kingdom of Heaven is eternal, all the Sons of Gods in the kingdom of Heaven are unified and the same, which makes every Son of God in the kingdom of Heaven share the memory of "I was the first one created by God in the beginning". So in the kingdom of Heaven, every Son of the God can't tell who is the first one to be created. It's like cell division. Cell A divides into Cell B, and A says that it divides into B. However, B can also say that he divides into A. Therefore, all the Sons of God in the kingdom of Heaven have a common awareness and recognition, that is, each of them thinks that he is the first one to be created, and he also creates an unlimited number of other Sons of God.

After describing the appearance of Heaven, let's talk about what happened later: when the infinite number of Sons of God are in the same Heaven, you (one of the infinite number of Sons of God) enter the dream. After entering the dream, you become the pure consciousness, then the subconscious, and finally you project the universe.

As you project the universe, you become a body. When you become a body, you start to wander in your dream. Then when you wander, you learn something. After that, you begin to distrust the big dream of the universe. For example, after you learn "A Course in Miracles", you begin to practice miracle minds. At the end of the practice, you experience awakening. At the moment of your awakening, you will recall the most ancient memory: you are the first Son created by God. So the awakening experience is just a real reappearance of memory. In this reappearance, your mind will change into spirituality and be in God. Then you will truly feel again how you, the first Son of God was created by God. Then, when you feel the whole process of being created, your awakening experience will end. So in the awakening experience, you will not perceive the existence of other Sons of God, because the awakening experience is only the most ancient memory, and the "after" of this memory is that other infinite number of Sons of God are created at the same time. So in the awakening experience you cannot perceive that the infinite number of other Sons of God in the same God with you. That's why "A Course in Miracles" says that "awakening is also an illusory experience, and only a part of awakening experience is real experience".

Then, when you experience awakening, you will return to the body, and then you will experience some years of enlightenment. In this period, you will understand that all people can awaken just like you, and all people are Sons of God and live in the kingdom of Heaven together. At this time, your preparations for a complete return to the kingdom of Heaven (breaking away from reincarnation) are "ready". At last, when you come to the last moment when you abandon your body in your dream, you will directly enter the kingdom of Heaven where an infinite number of Sons of God is unified and together, and then you will be fully activated. And at this moment, you are not the only one who is activated, because at the moment of your complete return, you will confirm that other infinite number of Sons of God have never left the kingdom of Heaven, at this time, other infinite number of Sons of God will be activated by your return. This is what "A Course in Miracles" says: when you come back, you come back together with the infinite number of Sons of God. So the moment when you return to Heaven thoroughly, you and all Sons of God will have the following awareness (the awareness of being activated) at the same time: we (I) seem to have had a dream, we (I) also seem to have entered the dream, but at this moment, in the eternal Heaven, the dream completely disappeared. Gee, it's interesting, but it's a total nonsense.

Well, I've finished the whole process of "things". The end of this process is that all the Sons of God are "activated", so when you have broken away from the reincarnation, you will never enter any dream again.

Q: Hearing your reply, I have become confident in my practices. Thanks!

A: You can understand the whole question in combination with the auxiliary answer just now. That's the only way to answer your question. But even if this question is answered, it may not help others, because the answer to this question is only an external explanation for the practitioner. So the key question is whether you can trust the truth within you. However, the truth inside you can only be trusted by you through your own practice. This is the general position of the practitioner. So it depends on your own choice whether you can "confront the difficulties".

Finally, if you want to ask, "how did the kingdom of God come from? What was it before the advent of God?" There is no answer to this question, because Heaven has neither "before" nor "after".

44

Q: Is dream the projection of the guilt in subconscious? Do we need to be aware of and forgive it? Or is everything meaningless and doesn't need to be analyzed?

A: Do you mean dreaming at night? If so, there is no need for too much forgiveness. Night dreaming is only a shallow projection of the subconscious.

Q: Is it better to release fear in a dream? Otherwise, it can't be detected because it is hidden in it (although in fact, the dream at night and the experience during the day are not real, they are all dreams).

A: Oh, let me give you an example. For example, you are afraid of divorce, but you often practice for divorce, for example, you often entrust the fear of divorce. At this time, if one day you dream of your divorce, it proves that your fear of divorce has been released. So for a miracle practitioner, the dream you have at night is probably a sign that fear has been released, which is a good thing.

45

Q: Does everyone need to pass the same exercises of practicing?

A: Everyone's exercises of practicing are different. But the practitioners do experience the same practicing situation along the way. This situation is that everyone will practice repeatedly and perennially for a certain period of time, so that he can complete a larger life task. For example, some practitioners in this Wechat group need to practice repeatedly for their husbands' attacks, some for their wives' sacrifices, some for their elders' behaviors all year round, and others for their loneliness at present. This is a situation that all the practitioners have to experience. And the experience of this situation also represents that the practitioner is getting through a relatively large "mind block" in his mind. At this time, his state of mind will go up to a higher level due to the opening of the block and continuous learning.

From a certain point of view, the larger life topic is the key to practice, followed by learning. Because the things that can hinder your mind growth are actually those big "mind blocks", so opening these blocks is the basis for your further understanding of miracle wisdom. It's like this: if "A Course in Miracles" is a perfect medicine that can cure your mind, the premise and guarantee that this medicine can flow through the "whole mind" is that those big blockages in your mind are opened.

46

Q: I've heard you say that peace can be given by initiative. Can you tell me more about it?

A: It's a kind of advanced miracle mind to actively give peace. In terms of actual practice, active peace giving is a dynamic exercise based on many miracle minds. For example: a core member of your family, who has mental or physical illness, often loses his temper to you because of his illness, and he often loses his temper to you in front of others. In the face of this family member, you have seriously practiced miracle minds. For example, you know that he is only a patient, and every time he loses his temper, it is only a kind of sincere plea for help, because he just wants to get more care. So in the face of such a patient, every time you practice true forgiveness, giving purity and innocence, satisfying the other party's sincere plea for help (taking care of him in various ways), asking nothing in return and overcoming sacrifice. Then you will constantly entrust the following fears: if one day, I go out with him to have dinner with others, and he gets angry with me again in front of others, then I accept it, I accept it, because that situation is just a dream, it doesn't exist, and I'm not the victim of that situation. At this time, from the perspective of actual practice, you actually have practiced a lot of miracle minds perfectly. However, if you and him really go to a dinner party until one day, then if you still fear that he will lose his temper to you in front of many other people, you can exercise to give peace actively in the process of attending the dinner party. The thinking mode of this practice is as follows:

1. If he lose his temper against me in front of others, I will continue to forgive and not fight back. Because what I think and do is just to prepare for the final peaceful ending.

2. If he loses his temper against me in front of others and asks me to leave this room and go to another room, I will forgive and accept the offer

at the same time, because what I think and do is also preparing for the final peaceful ending.

3. If he loses his temper against me in front of others, and they continue to dissuade him and ask me not to fight back, then I will silently forgive their interaction and keep not fighting back, because their interaction is also preparing for the final peaceful ending.

4. If he loses his temper against me in front of other people, they dissuade him and let me go to another room first to stay away, I will also accept other people's suggestions, because I will not prevent them from making some suggestions, which are just preparing for the final peaceful ending.

5. If he loses his temper against me in front of others and asks me to go to another room, I will go. Then, after I leave, if someone exchanges and persuades him, and finally asks me to return to the restaurant, I will accept the suggestions and return to the restaurant. Because I know this series of events are preparing for the final peaceful ending.

6. If I go back to my room and he loses his temper against me in front of me again, I will still forgive and not fight back. Because my repetitive thoughts and actions are still preparing for the final peaceful ending.

At this point, if you can handle the dinner according to the above thought and action, you will complete the dynamic exercise of giving active peace, and then the exercise will show you a safe ending that cannot be completely described in words. As an example, the end result is that all the people who attend the dinner party and your family members will succumb to your continuous inner peace, their wrong thinking will be corrected by the Holy Spirit at the same time, and then you will become a man of men in everyone's mind. At this time, other people will neither blame your family members nor think you are a victim, because other people can fully feel how powerful the immeasurable peace inside you is. This kind of power will not hurt anyone, but radiate the light of love others as yourself. So at this time, in addition to being unable to praise you accurately with words, other people will also have great respect for you.

This is the peaceful ending that you can finally get for everyone, and this ending will have a profound impact on your future.

However, it can be said that if you still use the old conviction mode to deal with the problem when you participate in the dinner, the dinner will end, but the end is: everyone will think you are still the victim full of resentment and fear.

When you are in a specific event with more participants, you not only need to practice all kinds of miracle minds led by true forgiveness in the process of this event, but also need to constantly confirm in the process of practice that the continuous peace within you will manifest a peaceful ending that can be shared by all participants of this event. At the same time, you have to constantly believe that the decisions made by some people involved in the event are all in preparation for the final peaceful ending, and their decisions are only an integral part of that ending. At this point, you won't stop someone from making a decision. At this time, you will no longer fear that some decisions made by some people will bring you bad results. At this point, your mind will be completely peaceful, which is to give peace actively.

47

Q: After a period of practice in accordance with Chapter 9 of your required readings, I feel that my illness has been alleviated. Then I would like to ask if my illness can be completely cured in a period of time?

A: I can answer your question in this way: in practice, the process of a person's practicing physical diseases with miracle minds is relatively vague, and the time span is also very large. The normal situation is: you will get sick constantly in your life, and then when you are a beginner of miracle practices, you are likely to use drugs to treat the disease first, and then "a little" miracle minds may play a role in curing your disease. But as time goes by, for example, 10 years later, you may be able to use "half" drugs and "half" miracle minds for diseases at the same time. Finally, it will be another 10 years before you are likely to use miracle minds on a "large scale" in cooperation with "a little" drugs. So from a practical point of view, there are only two important principles for you to cure all physical diseases in your life: 1. Full patience; 2. Flexible use of medical methods and miracle minds. Remember, "the useful is the best."

Although "A Course in Miracles" has said that you can stand up directly from the hospital bed. But this sentence is only said from the perspective of absolute monism, so this sentence is not the same as the actual practice, because the actual practice must be: un untrained mind accomplishes nothing, and exercises depends on time.

48

Q: I would like to share your required readings with a Taoist disciple I know. Is that ok?

A: Of course. If a person takes off the mask of religious belief, he is just a common person. Even if he can take off all masks, he will not break away from daily necessities and interpersonal relations. Therefore, the required readings can be shown to anyone, no matter what kind of religious belief he has.

49

Q: I'm a new comer. After entering the website and reading the required readings, I decided to practice miracle minds. Can you give me some suggestions in advance?

A: the misfortunes and blessings of life are almost instantaneous and unprepared, so you need not prepare to practice this set of Holy Spirit thought system. But only when you think about it in person and preferentially according to this system can the Holy Spirit be one with you. Therefore, the general proposal I can present is: "Heaven is running ceaselessly, so the gentleman shall improve himself continuously."

Appendix

Brief Notes to 50 Principles of Miracles and an Introduction to A Course in Miracles (ACIM)

In the required readings, I mentioned that the information I illustrated were all from "A Course in Miracles" and the series of "The Disappearance of the Universe", and the information that I illustrated were not beyond these two sets of books. This is the position held by me, the illustrator, and the information I illustrate. And the position can also show you that the information I state is only a step that can maximally enable you to understand "A Course in Miracles"(ACIM), the main textbook.

Besides, I, the illustrator deeply knows, if you want to maximally understand ACIM, you should first of all know how the thought system of ACIM is to be used in life, and you should also understand what benefits this thought system can bring you, then you will well maintain a will to learn ACIM. This is why my required readings came into being, and this is also why the series of "The Disappearance of the Universe" came into being.

Considering that you may directly read this appendix and the independence of this Appendix, I will use a practical case in the required readings as the introduction of illustrating ACIM and 50 principles of miracles, and I will briefly explain the general meaning of the name of ACIM again, and I will move into the stage of illustration.

The introduction is as follows:

A couple are both bread earners. One day the husband became infatuated with network games, he played games after work every day, which disgusted his wife. After some time, the wife got fed up with it, and she scolded her husband when he was playing games: "you play games every day and ignore me, you go live with the people in games if you play again! Turn off the computer now!" When the husband heard that, he got angry and replied, "What's wrong with me playing games after work? Don't manage me, don't make much ado about nothing." Then the wife got madder, and continued, "How long since you last accompanied me to shop? You should accompany to shop now, if you play again, I will smash the computer." Then the husband continued to flight back: "You can smash the computer, I will not go." At last the couple quarreled. And the case came to an end.

If you are the husband in the case, how should you think so that you can change the Ego thought that regards the world as real into another set of holy spirit thought that knows the world is a dream? Or, when you are in that situation, how should you think and do to acquire peace of mind and peaceful situation?

Then I will briefly narrate the thoughts and actions you shall practice:

First of all, you shall be alert that you have already regarded the world as real during the process of quarrel or after the quarrel. Then you can practice the following thought and carry out the actions:

Truly forgive your wife. You should realize that you are only in a dream and you dream of your wife and her body, so you only dream of yourself as a body in a dream, then you dream of an event of being attacked by your wife. So, the affair itself and she and I in the affair are illusions, and her self-consciousness and my self-consciousness are also illusions and do not exist.

2. Give the idea of innocence and guiltlessness to your wife. My wife is a mere spirit in heaven, she is pure and innocent. She has never left heaven, so the real her is an innocent idea, and she is not a body at all. Then you can experience that you yourself is but the idea of innocence and guiltlessness that you give away because of the power of true forgiveness and giving purity and innocence, for what you give away attest to what you own. So, when you have completed that step, you and your wife will be unified into a pure and innocent abstract idea, then the abstract idea will become a spiritual experience, and your spiritual experience cannot be molested or destroyed by the illusions. So that spiritual experience is a miraculous state

230

of mind that is safe and beyond the dreamland, which is what the course intends to express. Only the miraculous state of mind at that time is only an embryo or an incomplete body for that matter.

3. Practice giving up two demands. 1. You should realize that your fondness of computer games is because you want to fill the sense of deprivation within you with the sense of satisfaction brought by the games. But the problem is, you only reside in a dreamland, so if you affirm that the sense of satisfaction of playing games is real, the world will become real. At the same time, the sense of deficiency inside you will be real in your mind. But, if the deficiency inside you becomes real, you can no longer fill that deficiency that has become real with anything in the dream. Because the world either becomes real with the deficiency, or becomes illusory with the deficiency. So, as the husband in the case, what you should do is to realize the deficiency within you is illusory, and you are able to dissolve that deficiency by abandoning the action of playing games. 2. You shall be aware that, if you want your wife to permit you to play games, you still want to change your wife into a person that can satisfy your deficiency, so that thought and the action of counter-attack (the act of asking her to change) is also a manifestation of taking deficiency seriously. So, in the same sense, if you want to dissolve the "same" deficiency, you should abandon the thought of "changing the wife", and achieve that by no-retaliation.

When you have abandoned those two demands and dissolved the deficiency, the embryo of the miracle mind you have just owned and become will be strengthened by you and become a miracle mind without deficiency. At that time the fear that your wife holds that you may get addicted to playing games will be dissolved, and she will no longer attack you. For the attack your wife exerts on you will disappear because of the disappearance of her fear, and the world is dreamt of you, so the fear that disappears will not be outside of you.

4. Practice satisfying genuine plea for help. You should think that, my wife generates deficiency because she is in want of a husband who can accompany her, then she asks me to be a person who can often

231

accompany her due to deficiency, so that demand can also be said to be her call for help. The problem is that the world is a dream projected by my sub-consciousness, so the deficiency of my wife is also within my sub-consciousness. Only this time the "same" deficiency is represented by a body outside my body. So, if I want to dissolve "the same" deficiency within my sub-consciousness, I shall first of all transform and define the deficiency as illusory, then I can dissolve that. Then how can I carry out this transformation and dissolution? That is, I shall use my time and energy to satisfy her deficiency, that is to use the action of shopping to satisfy her call for help. Just this time, when I satisfy her deficiency, I shall think simultaneously, or, I shall clearly realize that the energy and time I spend accompanying her to go shopping is illusory before or during the action, so I am not afraid to lose these illusory things, and I am willing to do so. At that time, "the same" deficiency within your sub-consciousness will be transformed into an illusory one and directly dissolved. This is the content and form of satisfying other people's call for help, only that actions shall be matched with this thought system.

When you can satisfy other people's call for help, the deficiency within your wife will vanish, while her fear that you will never accompany her will also be partially dissolved. Up to now, the miracle mind you have just owned and become will again be completed to a non-deficient miracle mind featuring loving others as oneself. The meaning of "loving others as oneself" is: when you interact with another person, you are able to see his truth and your truth through his illusory body, you are also able to deal with the specific problems in your life according to a thought system based on the idea that the world is only a dream, and also able to dissolve the manifestation of deficiency and fear of others. This is the real connotation of "loving others as oneself". This connotation also represents that you are able to lead others by example through expressing:" I am the Son of God, I ask for nothing, and I lack nothing, and I will not be restrained and bound by anything in the dream." This is a connotation of "teaching and learning" and "learning and teaching" mentioned by this course.

5. Practice facing fear (entrusting fear). When you have completed the above practices, you may still keep some fear left. To be specific, the fear

is that you will fear that your wife will continually ask you to abandon some demands, or fear that she will continually ask you for some help. So, when this fear appears, you may think like that: Even if those things I am unwilling to experience happen in the future, I accept it, I accept it. For even if those things would happen, only a dream happens and nothing truly exists, so even if they would happen, they cannot influence my truth and I will calmly face them and experience them, and I will never be the victim of those things.

When you entrust fear like that, the miracle mind you have just owned and become will again be completed to a non-deficient miracle mind featuring loving others oneself and fearlessness. Up to now, you have finally completed and accomplished the miracle mind in a specific affair. A specific problem or a specific trouble in your life has been thoroughly removed by the thoughts you have used. Then your mind will experience eternal peace. And that eternal peace is the main feature of miracle mind.

At last, when you have experienced that eternal peace, that peace will immediately or gradually manifest a peaceful situation to you. For instance, this peaceful situation is: your wife will gradually let go of her attack and restraint on you because you continuously practice miracle minds. The fear that she worries about your addiction to network or becoming the person that does not accompany her will disappear completely. Then she will trust you more and more and express a harmonious feeling towards you. And that harmonious feeling will be captured by your self-consciousness. This is the side benefit you will obtain.

Then what are the main benefits of your practicing the aforementioned thoughts? That is to awaken to your own truth. That answer will pull out the general connotation of "A Course in Miracles": This is a course that narrates miracle minds and will transform you into a miraculous state of mind. This course develops from the truth that you are the Son of God and the world is a dream, and it can comprehensively transform your thought system to regard the world as real into another thought system that realizes that the world is a dream. And all the thought patterns narrated by the course will be combined and applied to every specific problem in your life, so you can remove every problem in your life yourself and incessantly become a peaceful miraculous state of mind. And the spiritual experience of miraculous mental state also resembles your truth: the enlightenment that the Son of God resides within Heaven eternally. If you are often able to experience yourself to be a miraculous state of mind, that "quantitative change" will be transformed into "qualitative change" at a certain moment, then you will awake from your dream of life and will wake up within God. This is the main benefit ACIM and the miraculous state of mind will bring you. While miraculous mental state will bring you two side benefits: 1. Miraculous state of mind will greatly shorten the time you wander in the dream. 2. Miraculous state of mind will manifest peaceful experience. Those are the general meaning of ACIM.

Then, I have to remind you of two points before I explain ACIM:

1. No one will force you to learn this course. For the vitality does not come from the world you have dreamt, but from Heaven within your mind, and it is only a book in the world. So, whether you learn or not depends on your choice.
2. The practices of every step in the introductory case will purify your mind in a certain sense. That is to say, even if you only achieve true forgiveness (the first practice) in some specific problem, you will get a corresponding purification of mind. So, when you combine and apply miracle minds towards a specific affair, the more correct you apply, your mind will get better purified.

A Course in Miracles (ACIM)

INTRODUCTION

T-in.1. I will explain the introduction of ACIM with simple Chinese:

1. This is a course that illustrates miracle minds and makes you a miraculous state of mind.

2. The reason that the course is called a compulsory course, is because the ideas the course narrates are trials that every person who walks in the course of enlightening shall experience. Even if you do not awaken in God through ACIM, you have been bound to walk the path of practicing many important ideas illustrated in the course. Even if those ancient spiritual practitioners who had returned to Heaven did not read ACIM, they had practiced some important ideas in ACIM without exception. So, this course is a compulsory heavenly script defying time and space.

3. The time you devote to the course is optional, you may learn it when you want to learn it, the duration of your learning is up to you. And you probably learn it on and off crossing transmigration.

4. and 5. No one can force you to learn this course, for your free will is bestowed upon you by God, so your free will and your own right to choose is the biggest. However, your right of free learning and your ability to understand the course completely are two different stories. So, the normal situation is that: if you can practice all the miracle minds narrated in ACIM continuously for many years, you may probably understand this course. Therefore, you shall not think that to understand this holistic and holographic book is easy. Certainly, you may learn a certain miracle mind and apply it to a specific matter during a period of time, for this kind of intermittent learning is also your freedom.

6. and 7. The student of the course is not you in Heaven, for your truth, that is the Son of God is unshakeable, needs no schooling, and cannot be educated. Nevertheless, the Son of God has entered a dream and taken the dream seriously, and the thought system that regards the world as real is the barrier to keep the Son of God from experiencing himself to be the Son of God. So, the student of the course is but the illusory "you" who

has not yet experienced himself to be the Son of God. The objective of this course is only aiming at dissolving "your" thought system that regards the world as real. Certainly, no matter how long "you" wander in the dream, or whenever "you" begin to practice this course or how long you practice the course, those will not impact the truth that you are the Son of God and eternally reside within God.

8. This sentence has two connotations: first, Love represents you have correctly combine and apply various miracle minds to deal with that problem and become miraculous state of mind, Love comes into being from this complete peaceful miraculous state of mind, therefore, though the opposite of love is fear and illusion, wherever Love is present, fear and illusion will lose their meaning, this is the reason why Love has no opposition. Second, Love represents Heaven of God. Within Heaven, there is no room for fear and illusion, so Heaven has no opposition.

T-in.2.

1. Therefore, this course can be briefly summarized as:

2. Only Heaven of God really exists, and your dream cannot intrude into Heaven, so Heaven is not menaced at all. Besides, the miraculous state of mind that you can become is also beyond dreamland, so it cannot be menaced. However, the miraculous state of mind is like a raft taken to cross the river, and when you return to Heaven, it will lose its meaning and will disappear.

3. The body bound to your self-consciousness is a subject, and the object this is opposite to the subject is the world before your eyes and sentient beings in the world. However, both the subject and the object are a dream of you, the son of God, so both the subject and the object are illusory and have never existed.

4. The miracle mind and the peaceful miraculous state of mind come into being from the two aphorisms that are able to summarize the truths.

Chapter 1

THE MEANING OF MIRACLES

I. Principles of Miracles

T-1.I.1.

The first principle needs to be illustrated by inserting a small case and comparing the case with the introductory case.

The case is as follows:

When you discussed some ideas of ACIM with others online, an anonymous netizen emerged, abused and personally attacked you. How shall you practice when you are in that kind of situation?

1. You shall realize in your thought: I just dream of "an event in which I am anonymously insulted", I only dream of that netizen and his body, so I only dream of myself as a body. So, this affair and he and I in the affair are all illusions. Besides, his self-consciousness and my self-consciousness are all illusions and do not exist.

2. Giving the idea of purity and innocence to that netizen: he is only a spirit within Heaven, he is pure and innocent, he has never left Heaven, so the true he is merely a pure and innocent idea.

At that time, when you have completed the two steps of practices mentioned above, you will experience that you are only a pure and innocent idea that you have given away owing to the power of true forgiveness and giving away purity and innocence. At that time, your spirit will experience peace beyond everything, and you have become a complete embodiment of the miraculous state of mind.

At last you can achieve the mental affirmation mentioned above by refraining from counter-attack. Up to now one of your specific problems has been dissolved.

The case has been finished.

By the comparison between the case and the introductory case, you can realize that, the number of the miracle minds you respectively combine and apply to those two affairs are different, but the final result they lead to is the same, that is the complete embodiment of the miraculous state of mind. This is the connotation of "miracle" in this principle. In this principle, "miracle" represents the miraculous state of mind. So miraculous state of mind do not have any order of difficulty, or any order of size, for they are the same mental state and the same matter.

The last sentence of this principle is to say, if you can correctly apply some miracle minds to deal with some specific matters for many years, you will continuously lead all the people by example of expressing true love, because love is born in nothing but peace, while peace is born in nothing but the miraculous state of mind, and the miraculous state of mind is born in miracle minds headed by true forgiveness. This is the connotation of the last sentence of this principle.

Certainly, in this dream, you really need to continuously combine many miracle minds to solve a specific problem. In terms of this point, the combined application of miracle minds may be more or fewer. But the thing is, you only apply more or fewer miracle minds in a dream, so no matter how many you have applied miracle minds, no matter how many problems you have solved, or no matter how many times you have become the miraculous state of mind, they are only a course of spiritual practicing that does not exist.

T-1.I.2.

Miracle minds and miraculous state of mind are insignificant themselves, because they are draw-boards for your awakening within God. Besides, the only really existent domain is God's Heaven. So, when you use these two instruments to return to God's Heaven, those two instruments will lose their meaning and disappear into the void, that is the reason for the insignificance stated in this principle. However, they are insignificant for Heaven, yet they originate from God, because they are the voice of waking you up from God. So, their value is beyond dream and cannot be evaluated by any ideas in the dreamland.

T-1.I.3.

This principle is briefly annotated as: 1. Peaceful situation is manifested by miracle minds. 2. So the key question is that whether you can correctly practice miracle minds and achieve the miraculous state of mind. 3. For miraculous state of mind is the fountainhead of peaceful situation of miracle.

T-1.I.4.

In God's Heaven, you will be eternally aware that you are a spirit residing within God, you are one with God, you are also one with God along with other countless spirits, the whole Heaven is your noumenon. While you practice miracle minds in the world and become the real world, you will experience that you and all people are merely a unified idea that is pure and innocent. So, the spiritual experience of the Real World closely resembles the awareness that you reside in Heaven. Therefore, the Real World is filled with lives that resemble those within Heaven.

The second sentence of the second principle is to say that, if you are able to often practice miracle minds in the world and obtain more purifications, there will arise in your mind more correct inspirations. And those inspirations will prompt you to complete more advanced practices and until a moment at last, God will personally draw your mind into his heavenly mind, then you will awaken within God and affirm that the world before your eyes does not exist at all.

T-1.I.5.

This principle distantly corresponds with your truth. As a Son of God residing in dream, you shall foster the practice of miracle minds to be a habit. You shall not determine which things need practicing miracle minds, and which things do not need that. Because there is nothing in the dreamland that you, the son of God cannot forgive. Certainly, the requirement of this principle is very high, and is not what a beginner can achieve. Besides, the official, business and legal domain really have a set of rigid and fixed rules, which really restrain the number of illusions you can get, and the legal domain can also restrain the freedom of body. So, this principle only widely applies to private matters and the domain of interpersonal relationship.

T-1.I.6.

As a son of God residing within God, the course that you practice miracle minds and become miraculous state of mind and finally return to Heaven is a natural experience. Yet when you take the dream seriously all along, you will continually wander in the dream and incessantly experience birth, aging, sickness and death.

T-1.I.7.

As a son of God residing in dream, you are able to achieve continuous and perfect practicing correct miracle minds towards all things. This is the talent you yourself possess. Yet, if you want to reach that high-standard state, it requires you to take time and perseverance. Then with the passing of time and implementation of practices, your mind will be incessantly purified, and finally you probably will become a perfect practitioner.

T-1.I.8.

This principle is to narrate that a person who practices miracle minds will cause what kind of influences over himself and others. You may refer to my required readings to understand it. This time I only use the introductory case to illustrate it. The husband in the introductory case dissolved the deficiency, guilt and fear within his sub-consciousness by using the miracle minds, and at that time he was the relatively wealthier. At the same time, his practice also dissolved the deficiency and fear of his wife, his wife also felt the peace within him, and the deficiency of his wife was made up.

T-1.I.9.

This principle narrates that, the expression of Love equals to your practicing miracle minds in the world. And miracle mind has a very important feature, that is, you will obtain and become what you have given away. In terms of the introductory case, the husband achieved self-forgiveness when he forgave his wife (giving away forgiveness). Then, he became guiltlessness when he gave away purity and innocence. That is a very important feature of miracle mind, to give away is to possess. So, that pattern transcends the natural law in the world that when you give away something, you lose something. So, that pattern will not only enable the giver to own what he has given away, it also enables the receiver to obtain comforts of the mind.

T-1.I.10.

Miracle mind is only an intangible wisdom that enables people to return to the truth promptly, miraculous state of mind is also only an intangible spiritual experience, while peaceful situation is only a beautiful illusion, and the world is what you dream of. So, ACIM has only one reader, that is you. Therefore, the important point is whether you are able to practice miracle minds, not whether other people are able to practice miracle minds. In other words, if you force another person to learn miracle mind, you have regarded the suffering of another person as real, then you will lose your own peace firstly. Besides, if you think that people who practice miracles are different from others that do not practice miracles, you will fall into the trap of specialness. Because ACIM is written for everybody, and the circle of miracles is only a formless binding.

In sum, if you want to benefit others by miracle minds, you shall only hold this mental state: I may share my experience of practicing with others, but I will not take their drawing on that experience or not drawing on that experience seriously.

T-1.I.11.

This principle can be understood by referring to the chapter 'True Prayer and Wealth' of 'The disappearance of the Universe". The state of true prayer enables you to ceaselessly deepen your belief that you are the Son of God, and this deepening is kind of "approaching" God and "Communion" with God. So, the belief that you are the Son of God will be ceaselessly deepened. Then you will more alertly walk on the course of practicing miracle minds.

T-1.I.12.

1. The miracle minds headed by true forgiveness is only a set of thought pattern.

2. and 3. The miraculous state of mind resulting from miracle minds is a spiritual experience, which closely resembles the awareness that you reside within Heaven of God, so the miraculous state of mind is an experience of spiritual level you may become and experience. Yet, if your self-consciousness regards the world as true, your sense organs will sense a material image world, then your mind will experience "lower level" heartfelt feelings such as deficiency, guilt, fear, etc. Certainly, the "lower" and "higher" in this principle are only a kind of analogy, for the lower level and higher level in this principle do not have intersection.

T-1.I.13.

1. and 3. Practicing miracle minds is the beginning of the last lesson of your life, and is also the bugle call predicting that the world is to be terminated and dissolved. For practicing miracle minds can shorten the time you take to awaken from the dream, and it can also terminate past mistakes you have committed and dissolve the re-emergence of a mistake

in the future. Take the introductory case as an example, if you as the husband fail to act according to miracle minds, matters with the same connotation will appear again in your future, and then you have to choose whether you shall use a set of alternative thought patterns to deal with that matter again. That is to say, you used to choose mistakenly in the past, so the matter with the same connotation happen again today, and give you an opportunity to choose again. Therefore, practicing miracle minds can undo everything in the "past" at "present", hence liberating the "future".

2. Becoming the miraculous state of mind is the last segment of heartfelt feeling in your life dream, and it is also the spiritual experience that the world is to be terminated and dissolved. Besides, the miraculous state of mind can also pave the way for your resurrection, i.e., enlightenment. The experience of awakening seems that you return to God's Heaven from the dream, it seems that you return to when time begins. Nevertheless, when you become the peaceful miraculous state of mind within the linear time, that peaceful spiritual experience actually points forward along with time, then that kind of peace will be transformed to the safety in Heaven at the moment that you lay down the body for the last time and return to Heaven. Finally, that safety will accompany you, the Son of God until eternal eternity. This is the meaning of "moving forward all along" in this principle.

You may refer to the series of "The disappearance of the Universe" for more connotations of this principle.

T-1.I.14.

This principle may be understood referring to the 4th and 5th principle. Miracle mind and miraculous state of mind testify to your truth, while your truth guarantee miracle mind and miraculous state of mind, while your belief in the truth definitely come from within you, too. Therefore, those three dimensions will strongly be persuasive for your self-consciousness. Yet, you shall pay attention to one point, when you have practiced miracle minds, when you have achieved miraculous state of mind and peaceful situation, you shall never ever use those "achievements" to ask for something from others, you shall not use those "achievements" to let others accuse themselves. To put it more plainly, that is, please do not say to others: "If it were not for my practicing miracles for so many years, how can our family be so peaceful?" or "I have done so many things that you fail to do, why do you stir up troubles?" For those words represent that you are exchanging the truth for illusions, while words like that have profound specialness and sense of sacrifice. Therefore, those words represent that you treat miracle mind and peaceful situation as a stake that can obtain other illusions. At that time, miracle minds and peaceful situations have become your magic. At the same time, you will fall into a state of practicing not based on the truth, which is a mindless state. Certainly, that mindless state will damage your mind, for it is the committer of transforming creative ability into the ability to make illusions after the Son of God enter the dream.

T-1.I.15.

This principle is a kind of encouragement. It encourages you to caution yourself and practice miracle minds on certain things. So, tine is an instrument for the process of your practicing miracle minds. Then time will disappear at the moment of your returning to Heaven.

T-1.I.16.

The note of this principle is quite similar to that of the ninth principle, and one sentence can be added: practicing miracle minds in interpersonal relationship will ceaselessly purify the mind of you, the practitioner, while people around you will get more consolations from your practicing, then your interpersonal relationship will get more harmonious, finally you will ceaselessly see vitality in your interpersonal relationship.

T-1.I.17.

The miraculous state of mind is a kind of unified, unitary, intangible and peaceful spiritual experience, which transcends the world before your eyes and transcend your body. It can dissolve the sins and guilt within your sub-consciousness and dissolve your sub-consciousness. While all your psychological diseases and physical diseases originate from your sub-consciousness and sins and guilt within your self-consciousness. So, miraculous state of mind has the power of healing.

T-1.I.18.

Miracle minds and miraculous state of mind is a supreme affirmation that you the practitioner can give others. You will become what you affirm other people to be. This is called "loving another person as oneself". You may understand it by referring to the narration in the introductory case.

T-1.I.19.

Within Heaven of God, you are eternally unified with boundless spirits, you know each other that all of you is one life. Besides, you know each other that you will eternally reside within God. This is the awareness that the Son of God resides in Heaven. And miracle mind or the real world is a spiritual experience that most resembles that awareness. So, miracle mind transcends time, and have the characteristic of eternity. Certainly, that eternal characteristic can only be known by you through your own practices.

T-1.I.20.

Practicing miracle minds and becoming miraculous state of mind enable the practitioner to realize himself to be an intangible spiritual existence, and the practicing will ceaseless dissolves the guilt within your sub-consciousness. Then your mind will be ceaselessly remedied. Then until the very last, you will awaken to your truth at a certain moment of the linear time, then you will affirm that you are but Son of God, you are only a spirit and reside on the central point within God, and you are the altar of the truth.

T-1.I.21.

1. Miracle minds are headed by true forgiveness, so the acquisition of miraculous state of mind cannot do without the thought pattern of true forgiveness.

2. When you practice miracle minds, you are bound to practice the thought of true forgiveness first, but whether you forgive yourself by forgiving others, or you forgive all people by forgiving yourself, are all called extending forgiveness to people. All those signal that you have received the forgiveness of God. Certainly, receiving the forgiveness of God is only a worldly verbal expression, which only represents that God firmly will you, Son of God is able to wake up from dream. So, that expression does not represent that there is some distance and estrangement between you and God, for you and God has never been separated.

T-1.I.22.

1. This world is only an illusion projected by your sub-consciousness, even your eyes and ears have been projected by sub-consciousness. So, your eyes can only see illusory images, and your ears can only hear illusory sounds. This is the boundary that the function of bodies cannot go beyond. So, even if what you see is a sunny morning, it is only nothingness. In this principle, "darkness" represents this illusory world. Then this principle illustrates a normal experience, that is: when people regard this illusory world as real, people will think that some ultimate profound meaning is hidden in this illusory world, so people seek in this world ceaselessly. However, you are not able to get anything in this illusory world. This is the core connotation of "Seek, but not find". So, when people often seek and do not find, people will produce an uncertainty and suspicion about the world. Yet exactly at that time, people will easily categorize miracle mind and miraculous state of mind as another esoteric secret sought but not found. Then people will produce many surmises and doubts about this set of wisdom, this is called "terrible associations" in this principle.

2. If you believe this world is real, you will believe invisible things do not exist at all, this cognizance will let you lose all perception of the truth.

T-1.I.23.

The scope this principle covers is very wide, so I suggest you refer to the series of "The Disappearance of the universe" and my required readings to understand it. The purpose of my briefly annotating ACIM is to maximally lessen the difficulty of your understanding ACIM. Apart from this purpose, my notes and suggestions do not have other purposes.

T-1.I.24.

1. When you become a senior practitioner of all the miracle minds (whether you get enlightened or not), when the patient who pleas for your help trusts you in a great degree, you are really able to heal the physical disease of the patient or revive the dead through the deepest spiritual connection with the patient. Since it is you who dream of birth, aging, sickness and death of sentient beings, so the abilities of curing diseases and reviving others must be within you. Certainly, the state of mind narrated by this principle is very advanced, and cannot be achieved by general practitioners. (Note: the series of "The Disappearance of the Universe" has given a most authoritative explanation of this principle.)

2.and 3. These two passages are narration of the pure monism. You are the real miracle, that is, the Son of god. Apart from this truth, everything else does not exist. So, you can only create other boundless spirits along with God in Heaven. And another dimension of Heaven is thorough light. So, apart from creating other unified bright spirits and enjoying bliss of Heaven, you are not possible to do any other things.

T-1.I.25.

The understanding of this principle shall be carried out by focusing on "atonement", which has 3 categories of connotations in this principle:

1. On the course of your practicing miracle minds, you are certain to experience that everybody has forgiven you at a certain moment, for nobody resides outside Heaven. Then, you will experience that you and everybody is just a unified miraculous state of mind, and everybody has been atoned. Certainly, that feeling will ceaselessly emerge due to your ceaseless practicing miracle minds. This is one dimension of atonement.

2. When you make an example by long-term practicing miracle minds, your practice will ceaselessly affect people around you, then in the course of your practicing, perhaps you will preach miracle minds for other people. Then, because you have led by example, others are very likely to join in practicing miracle minds. Then people will achieve the same miracle minds. That is the process of atonement for linear time and everybody. So, the situation that in linear time, other people will ceaselessly join the rank of forgiving and ceaselessly merge into the same miraculous state of mind, is another dimension of mutually linked atonement.

3. Both your own atonement (the first item), and atonement of everybody in linear time (the second item) originated from the atonement which the holy spirit had completed at the moment when you entered the dream. Because the beginning of atonement came from: at the moment of your entering the dream, the holy spirit entered the dream together with you, then he instantly forgave all that you had projected, including the time you had projected, then he bestowed purity and innocence upon everything, this is what holy spirit had done completely. Then, when the holy spirit has completed this, he stays in your mind all along and waits all along for you to follow his example one day. This is how and why atonement may operate in all levels of time and the third generalized dimension of atonement.

T-1.I.26.

Fear really follows the you in the dream as the shadow follows the form, so many thought patterns in this set of miracle minds has the purpose of dissolving fear. The 5th practice in the introductory case is the simplified narration of dissolving fear.

T-1.I.27.

1. The 25th principle narrate the status and function of the holy spirit, but the fountainhead of the holy spirit is still God, for the holy spirit is sent by God to enter your dream, so the ultimate source of this set of miracle minds is still God. So, this set of thought system is only what God expect

of you, and he expects that you can wake up from the dream of life early. And when you practice this set of thought system, you convey the same expectation from God for every Son of God.

2. When you practice miracle minds headed by true forgiveness, you shall stress the route that forgiving others is the precondition for self-forgiveness. For in Heaven, you, the Son of God is born at the moment that God bestows everything he has as himself upon you, so this thought system that represents the truth takes as the principal thing that giving away equal to owning.

T-1.I.28.

When people regard the world as real, fear follows them as the shadow follows the form. So, the thought system that takes the world seriously can be called Ego, or the thought system of fear. So, the function of miracle minds is to dissolve this set of thought system of fear. However, miracle mind is after all an instrument, whose function is only paving the way for your enlightenment. So, "Revelation" represents the experience of enlightening, and you will thoroughly know all the connotations of fearlessness in the future experience of enlightening.

T-1.I.29.

1. Miracle minds come from the holy spirit, and the holy spirit comes from God, so when you practice miracle minds in the human world, you are praising God.

2. When you are practicing miracle minds, you are bound to affirm that other people are also sons of God, and affirm that they are pure and innocent. While innocence is also perfection, so your affirmation is a eulogy of God and all the creations of God.

3. Miracle minds and miraculous state of mind transcend the bodily level and will remove guilt in the sub-consciousness, while physical disease all come from the guilt in the sub-consciousness, so miracle minds has the ability of healing mind and body.

T-1.I.30.

Practicing miracle minds will enable you to experience that you and everybody is a conceptual entity that is intangible, pure and innocent. And the experienced state of conceptual entity closely resembles the awareness that the spirits reside within Heaven. So, when you are practicing miracle minds, you are ceaseless deepening the cognizance that you are merely an abstract conceptual entity. And this ceaseless deepening is a ceaseless "approach" to Heaven, and this "approach" will facilitate your experiencing enlightenment at a certain moment. Certainly, awakening from the dream cannot be achieved immediately, that really needs perseverance and time to achieve that.

To understand the adjustment of perceptual levels and the sequence of the beginning and the end, you are advised to understand them referring to the series of "The Disappearance of the Universe".

T-1.I.31.

1.and 2. When you practice miracle minds, both that you achieve self-forgiveness by forgiving others, and that you forgive everybody by forgiving yourself, are based on others and yourself being forgiven. So, when you forgive others and giving innocence and purity to them, you shall be deeply aware that, without the illusory images of brothers, you cannot practice true forgiveness and giving away purity and innocence. So, you should be grateful for the illusions and truth of Brothers, this is the feeling of gratitude in this principle. And because the truth of brothers is also Sons of God, so, the truth of yourself and theirs is "horizontal". So, you needn't hold them in awe, because the word "awe" can only be applied to God, the co-creator of all the spirits. So, you shall thank God because of the true features of Brothers.

3. Unified miraculous state of mind is affirming the purity and innocence of Sons of God, while purity and innocence is holy. When you have yet practiced miracle minds, you fail to see the holiness of you and everybody. This failure is merely temporary, for your dream has an end.

Certainly, the fastness and slowness of awakening from the dream is surely your decision and choice.

T-1.I.32.

1. You are the person who can practice miracle minds and become the miraculous state of mind. When you lead people in practicing miracle minds in interpersonal relationship by example, you are displaying your common truth for other people. Then other people are bound to be affected by your displaying truth. This is the meaning of "praying for others".

2. Miracle minds affirm your holiness, and miracle mind is a substitution for Ego thought system.

3. The miraculous state of mind is a spiritual experience, which transcends every spiritual experience you may own in this world.

4. You, the spirit residing with Heaven is always impeccable and eternally blissful.

T-1.I.33.

This principle at first does a personified treatment of miracle minds and miraculous state of mind:

1. Because you are lovable and respectable Son of God, so miracle minds and miraculous state of mind all along wait for you and is willing to serve you, and this is how they show respect to you.

2. They can help you dissolve your self-consciousness, and find the light of truth within you, for one dimension of Heaven is pure light. While the miraculous state of mind has the characteristic of light.

3. Miracle minds can change your mistaken thought, and awake you from dream.

4. Miracle minds may remove all the restraint of the illusory world over you. At the same time, your mind will experience the peace of God.

T-1.I.34.

You may refer to the introductory case to understand why miracle minds and miraculous state of mind is a perfect protection.

T-1.I.35.

This principle can be understood referring to the first principle. Then this principle also stresses that miracle mind is only an intangible thought system, and miraculous state of mind is only an invisible spiritual experience, so they are not apparent.

T-1.I.36.

The miracle mind is of course the most correct thought pattern for the Son of God who takes the dream seriously. So, Miracle mind can revise all mistaken perception, and miraculous state of mind resembles the awareness that the Son of God resides within Heaven.

T-1.I.37.

This principle can be understood referring to required readings, which not only narrates how to use miracle mind to defuse mistaken thought, and also narrates how you should correctly combine various miracle minds to deal with a certain problem. While those narration can be practiced in the similar life scenes by drawing inferences about other cases. The fourth sentence of the principle is to say, when your thought and mind has undergone training for a long time, you will awaken in the truth.

T-1.I.38.

This principle can be understood referring to Principle 25 and Principle 27.

T-1.I.39.

1. Miracle minds can dissolve all mistaken thought, while miracle minds and miraculous state of mind all originate from the holy spirit.

2. The illusory world represents darkness, while miracle mind represents the light that dispels darkness.

T-1.I.40.

When you practice miracle minds in interpersonal relationship, you affirm that everyone is the unified, pure and innocent, abstract idea. "Abstract" refers to omni-presence. So, when you practice, you will feel that Heaven of God is that abstract, and omni-present.

T-1.I.41.

The miraculous state of mind is unified, while unity refers to integrity. While integrity represents that the individual is illusory. So, when your individuality has been substituted by miraculous state of mind, you will find that individuality is the initiator of the sense of deficiency.

T-1.I.42.

The meaning of this principle does not differ much from that of the previous principle.

T-1.I.43.

The brief note of this principle is: you understand the "miracle" in the principle as peaceful situation.

Miracle minds will orient spirits towards mental state of miracle (miraculous state of mind), and the miraculous state of mind will manifest miraculously peaceful situation, which is generally unexpected and to the satisfaction of all. This principle can be understood referring to the fifth chapter of required reading.

T-1.I.44.

In Heaven, you and countless spirits reside within the same God, and the holy spirit is also with you. This is called your Christ (Note: the holy spirit is the very same "mind" of all the spirits). Complete miraculous state of mind and the Real World also resemble your Christ. So, both your becoming complete miraculous state of mind or the Real world represent that you have affirmed your Christ.

T-1.I.45.

1. The moment when you mistakenly supposed that you have left Heaven and entered the dream, the holy spirit was sent by God to enter your dream, then the holy spirit forgave everything you have dreamt of and created a spiritual world quite different from the dreamland: the real world. When the holy spirit has achieved that step, he stays in your mind and patiently wait for you to follow his thought pattern one day. This is the reason why miracle mind and the miraculous state of mind never get lost.

2. The second sentence of this principle has two connotations: First, when you practice miracle minds towards somebody, the holy spirit will help you to revise some mistaken thought of that person to be positive. And his positive thought will at one moment affect those people around him that you do not know. To put it plainly, you practice miracle mind toward A, the consciousness of A will change positively, and that change will affect B, a friend of A, while B will also affect C. This is the connotation of the second sentence of this principle. Second, the world and the sentient beings of the world you have projected is but a manifestation of the guilt within your sub-consciousness, which can also be called an external symptom of your mental diseases. So, when you practice miracle minds, you are healing the guilt within your sub-consciousness and its external symptom. So, your practice will have healing effect for everyone in the world. To be specific, that effect is, your practice will shorten the time everyone wakes up from the dream. For example, you are a person who has just began practicing miracle mind, and you are an Indian, and on the other side of the world there is a Brazilian, whom you do not know, and he does not learn ACIM

for this lifetime, and he will not get to know you. However, because you practice miracle minds and become miraculous state of mind for many years, your practice will ceaselessly affect and change all the people in the world (only that the influence and change cannot be seen in the short term or by physical eyes, for those changes belong to the spiritual level). Then until one day, that Brazilian senses in the dark that he shall pursue something true at that moment, then he comes into a sphere of spiritual practices and encounters ACIM after several years. At last, at some miracle party, you meet him and become friends. The case is finished.

The instance I narrate is crude, but it can fully express the connotations of this principle. Besides, all connotations of this principle are elaborated in the series of "The Disappearance of the Universe", you may refer to it by yourself.

T-1.I.46.

The holy spirit is unified with God, while he enters your dream to complete the work of waking you up. So, the holy spirit is the medium of communication between you and God, and this also include the miracle mind of the holy spirit and the Real World he has prepared for you, all those are media of communication between you and God. However, those media of communication are only instruments by which you awaken in God. So, when you wake up, instruments will lose their function.

T-1.I.47.

1. and 3. The miraculous state of mind resulting from miracle minds transcends time and have eternity, and miraculous state of mind radiates to linear time sphere from outside of time. In other words, whenever you begin to practice miracle minds, the miraculous state of mind may let you understand that time is only an instrument, certainly that understanding entails a process of practicing.

This principle and the second sentence of this principle need to be explained briefly by a specific case in "The Disappearance of Universe". This case is the experience of Gary Renard's evading a car accident.

In "The Disappearance of the Universe", Pursah told Gary, just because you have practiced true forgiveness for many years, you were able to choose that late-exit film and forgave the bad film and finally watched it patiently the other day, then you were able to evade the car accident the other day. The connotation explained by this affair is: when you ceaselessly practice miracle minds, many previous guilts in your sub-consciousness will be ceaselessly dissolved, which result in the disappearance of adversity. And at the same time, the holy spirit will at the same time operate in your mind and give you some inspiration to do things right, which facilitate the change in your behavior and choice. At last, these changes will manifest a peaceful life situation for you to experience. This is the connotation of Gary's evading the car accident.

Besides, this connotation can be further extended to cause and effect of transmigration. It can be still illustrated by the event that Gary evaded the car accident. Gary's evading the car accident seems to be caused by practicing true forgiveness in this lifetime, But the inspiration the holy spirit gave to Gary is not only at the time of his choosing the film. For according to the idea of cause and effect in transmigration, Gary's car accident in this lifetime is related to some affairs of the previous lifetime.

Suppose that Gary was a cowboy in the west in the last lifetime. That cowboy used to injure another person when riding a horse, and the cowboy reproached himself, which would cause Gary to experience a car accident in this lifetime. However, Gary practices true forgiveness in this lifetime, then the holy spirit not only enters Gary's mind and gives him inspiration, but also entered the cowboy's mind and gave the cowboy some correct inspiration to transform his guilt to injure another person. In this case, the operation of the holy spirit is simultaneous and synchronous in both lifetimes of Gary. When the holy spirit simultaneously gives Gary and the cowboy inspiration, the cowboy would not be so guilty, and the experience of Gary's car accident would disappear. To put it more plainly, were not for Gary's practicing true forgiveness in this lifetime, he would certainly experience the car accident. While his previous reincarnation (the cowboy) must be a very guilty person after injuring another person. However, if Gary practices true forgiveness in this lifetime, he would certainly evade the car accident, for the holy spirit would not only give inspiration to Gary to choose a film, he would also enter the mind of the cowboy, and gave the cowboy some correct inspiration to dissolve his guilt. This is the means and the mode of operation of the holy spirit's changing your life experience, only that means and operation mode is very hard to be perceived by your self-consciousness, so it can be said to be a blind area of your self-consciousness. So, the holy spirit directly pointed out this mode of operation in "The Disappearance of the Universe". Then we can understand that your future life experience will be ceaselessly changed because you ceaselessly practice miracle minds. While the insight and mentality of your regarding things in your several previous lifetimes will be ceaseless revised due to your practices in this lifetime. This is the general connotation of the second sentence of this principle.

At last, the holy spirit's operation mode that transcends space and time and simultaneously and synchronously gives you inspiration also indicates that all of your transmigration and every lifetime of yours occurs at the same time, because time and space is originally a holographic illusion, and linear time is but an illusion of your self-consciousness.

T-1.I.48.

1. The essence of time is suffering. For time binds the illusory world, while time and space seem to you, the Son of God, an illusory cage. So, whether you are able to break out of prison depends on when you, the Son of God can practice this set of miracle minds.

2. The experience of Revelation and the experience of Enlightenment all have the characteristic of true eternity. You can refer to "The Disappearance of the Universe" for the experience of Revelation. The experience of Enlightenment cannot be described in words, and cannot be referred to. Besides, I the speaker suggest you the reader that, even if you get enlightened one day in the future, you shall not describe to anyone the elaborate experience and process of enlightenment. Because, if you describe the experience of enlightenment, others may say to you one day in the future: "That experience of yours is not enlightenment, but the experience I just experienced is enlightenment, instead." At that time, you would

realize that your previous describing the experience of enlightenment to others will cause negative impacts.

T-1.I.49.

This principle can be understood referring to the introductory case or comprehensively referring to required readings.

T-1.I.50.

The miracle mind can forgive all illusory things, and the miraculous state of mind resembles Heaven of God, your enlightenment is within that.

This is the end of the illustration of the introduction of ACIM and Section I of Chapter I.

Printed in the United States
By Bookmasters